Learning LIBRARY

Reading, Spelling, & Grammar

grade 4

The basic skills your 4th grader needs!

- *Reading Comprehension*
- *Dictionary Skills*
- *Sentence Structure*
- *Abbreviations*
- *Parts of Speech*
- *Capitalization*
- *Punctuation*
- *Possessives*
- *Root Words, Prefixes, Suffixes*
- *Synonyms, Antonyms, Homophones*
- *Similes, Analogies, Alliteration, Idioms*

Editor: Kathy Wolf
Contributing Writer: Rusty Fischer
Copy Editor: Tracy Johnson
Contributing Artists: Cathy Spangler Bruce and Sherry Neidigh
Typesetters: Lynette Dickerson, Mark Rainey
Cover Illustration and Design: Nick Greenwood

Table of Contents

Spelling

Vocabulary & Dictionary Skills

Grammar

Reading Comprehension

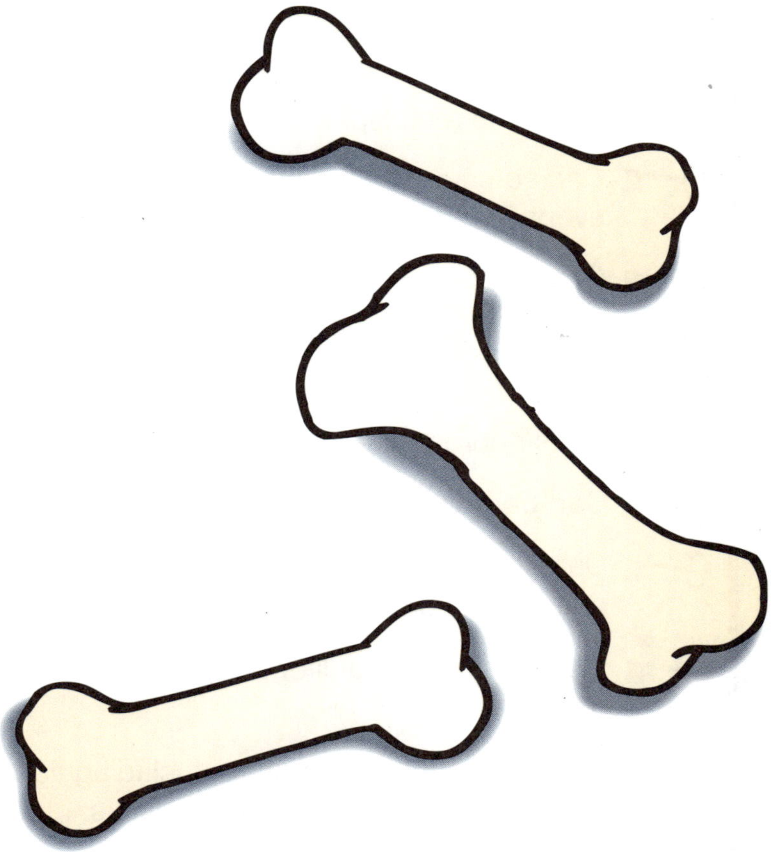

ISBN# 1-56234-483-8

Manufactured in the United States
10 9 8 7 6 5 4 3 2 1

Key Literacy Skills—Grade 4

- Uses knowledge of letter-sounds, language structure, and context to recognize words.
- Uses knowledge of root words to determine the meaning of unknown words.
- Can locate the meanings, pronunciations, and derivations of unfamiliar words using dictionaries, glossaries, and other sources.
- Uses knowledge of *word origins, derivations, synonyms, antonyms,* and *idioms* to determine the meaning of words and phrases.
- Can recognize words with multiple meanings and interpret figurative language as in *similes* and *metaphors.*
- Knows spelling of *root words, prefixes, suffixes,* and *verb tenses.*
- Can identify and use parts of speech: *nouns, pronouns, verbs, adverbs,* and *adjectives.*
- Uses appropriate *verb tenses, subject-verb agreement, pronouns, prepositional phrases*, and *conjunctions* in writing.
- Can capitalize and/or punctuate titles, possessives, and dates. Uses commas in a series, apostrophes, and appropriate ending punctuation.
- Can write a multiparagraph composition supporting a central idea.
- Can summarize the plot of a story, identifying major events, their causes, and how each event contributed to the conclusion.
- Can recognize and analyze the *plot, setting,* and *problem.*
- Can analyze a character's point of view, relationships, and changes, giving supporting evidence.
- Uses appropriate strategies when reading for different purposes.
- Can *paraphrase* and *summarize* to recall and inform.
- Can summarize and organize information from several sources by taking notes, outlining, and making charts.
- Identifies genres of literature, including biography, historical fiction, informational text, and poetry.
- Reads a variety of literature, including fiction (legends, novels, folklore, and science fiction), nonfiction (information books, autobiographies, diaries, and journals), poetry, plays, and myths.
- Uses prior knowledge, as well as information in the text, to make and confirm predictions and draw conclusions.
- Can distinguish between cause and effect and between fact and opinion.
- Can compare and contrast ideas, themes, and issues across readings.

Spelling

Your fourth grader will continue to build on his knowledge of spelling patterns, including common spellings of vowel sounds and consonant sounds. He will learn the spellings of common root words, prefixes, suffixes, and different forms of verbs. In addition, fourth graders are introduced to a lot of new "spelling rules." These spelling patterns involve the following:

- forming plurals with *-s* and *-es*
- adding *-ed, -ing, -er,* and *-est*
- doubling final consonants
- changing *y* to *i*
- dropping the final *-e*
- adding prefixes and suffixes

While it is imperative that fourth graders learn how to use these rules before progressing to fifth grade, teachers understand that all students advance at their own pace.

Fourth-grade teachers help students develop their "spelling consciousness" by addressing how children misspell words and giving them *spelling strategies* they can use to spell words that cause problems for them. These can include such tactics as

- thinking of rhyming words
- looking for problem parts
- pronouncing, then spelling
- dividing long words
- using memory tricks (To spell *arithmetic,* say, "A rat in the house might eat the ice cream!")

Students are encouraged to choose their favorite strategies to help spell troublesome words on their own. These strategies help children patrol their own spelling—a major focus in fourth grade! You can help your student spell better by choosing some of the activities at the bottom of the pages that you can do at home.

Trial and Error

A unique and fun way to improve your child's spelling at home is to make a game out of her weekly spelling tests. After reviewing the test and practicing misspelled words, ask your student to give the test—to you! Taking a cue from those misspelled words, spell some incorrectly and then let your "teacher" grade them. This is a great way for your fourth grader to see that everyone has trouble spelling, while at the same time gaining some additional confidence with those commonly misspelled words.

Name____

Clowning *A*-round

Zany Janie often gets confused. She thinks that if a word is spelled with an *ai*, *ay*, or *ei*, it always has the long *a* sound. Look at the words she has grouped inside the circus tents below. Write the word that doesn't have the long *a* sound below each group of words.

train
weigh
ceiling
stay

____

afraid
weird
neighbor
way

____

play
eight
receive
praise

____

explain
aisle
airplane
freight

____

Next, pretend you just went to the circus with Zany Janie and caught the clown act. Describe what you saw, using as many words with the long *a* sound as possible. Circle those words when you have finished.

____

____

____

____

____

____

____

Name____ Spelling: *ie*, *ee*, *ey*, *ea*

Check Your *E*mail

Jeannie wants to send her pal Pete an email. Read through it first and circle all the words with the long *e* sound that are spelled with an *ie*, *ee*, *ey*, or *ea*.

From: Jeannie27@email.com
To: Petey14@yourmail.org

Dear Pete,

My teacher took my class on a field trip yesterday. We went to a farm and fed the turkeys and chickens oats, grains, and peas. My friend and I got to hold a monkey. That was really neat. The weather was beautiful, so we stayed all day. When it was time to leave, no one wanted to go. Once we got on the bus, I put my head back and fell asleep. I had peaceful dreams of my great day!

Jeannie

Now it's your turn to send an email back, using as many words with the long *e* sound as possible. Underline your long *e* words when finished, and see if you can beat the number of long *e* words that Jeannie used!

Name ______________________________

Floating Down the River

Make a splash when you choose words with the long *o* sound that are spelled with *ow*, *oe*, or *oa* from the Word Bank. Use them to fill in the appropriate blanks in the river-rafting scene below.

Word Bank

	float	goat
boat	Joe	toe
row	coat	slow
know	grow	show
blow	goal	
flow	crow	

Now, use the remaining long *o* sound words (and a few of your own) to describe an adventure in a canoe. Underline the words that have the long *o* sound when you are finished.

____

____

____

____

____

Name____

The Eyes Have It!

Look at the creepy eyes below. Look for the *long i* sound. Color by the code. At the bottom of the page, write the appropriate words under the right color.

Code:
-ild = blue
-ight = yellow
-y = green

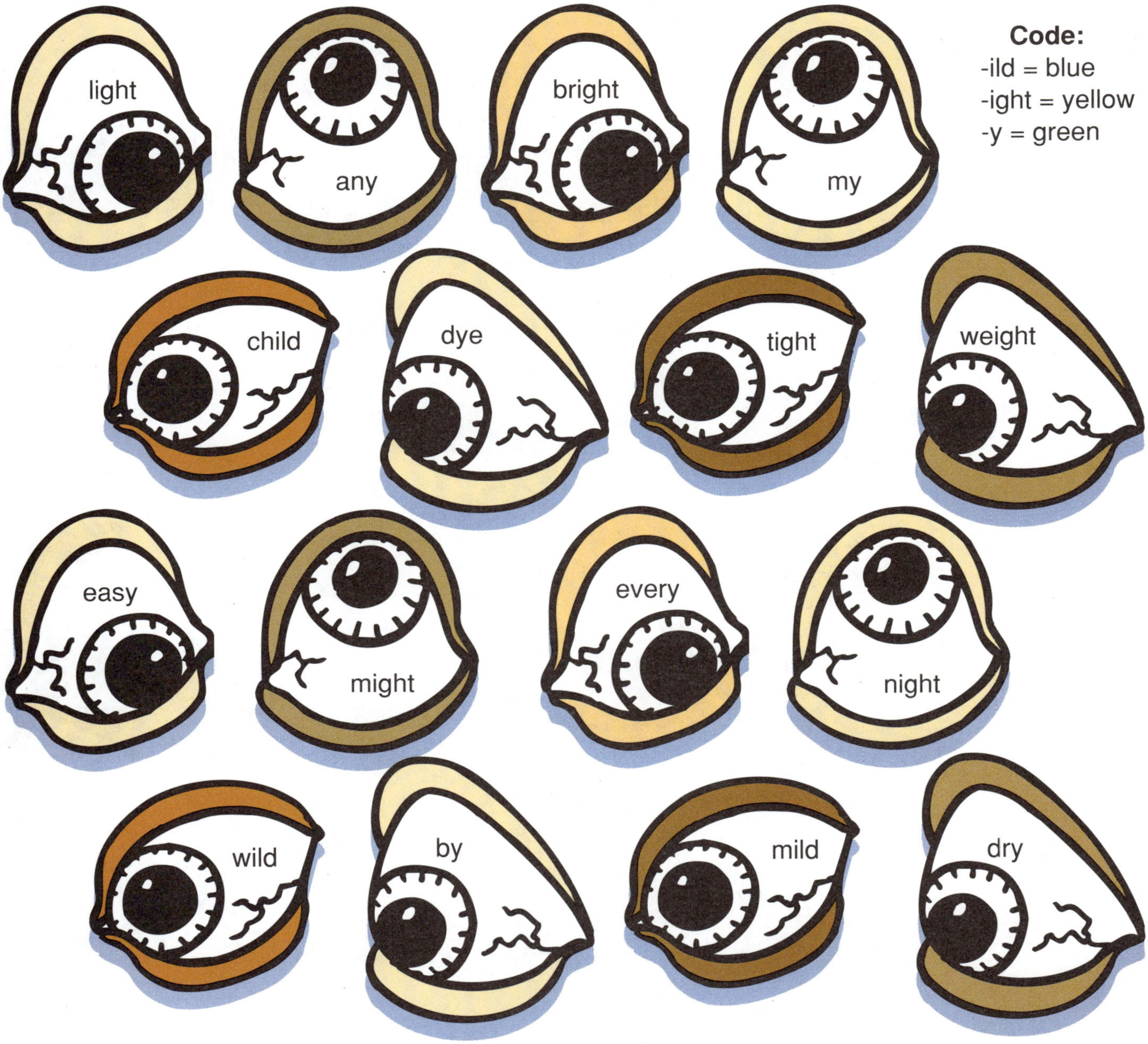

Blue Eyes	Yellow Eyes	Green Eyes	White Eyes
________	________	________	________
________	________	________	________
________	________	________	________
________	________	________	________
________	________	________	________

Name ______________________________ Spelling: *oo, ew, ui, ue, iew*

The Weather Report

In his weather report, Sailor Sam has used many words with the sounds of /ū/ as in rescue or /ü/ as in juice. Can you spot them? Fill in the blanks to complete the sentences with words from the word bank below.

It will not be __________ sailing for you boat lovers today. You'll have to __________ an indoor sport. It's __________ that winds __________ at 25 knots this morning and will __________ to blow even stronger as the day wears on. So, no __________ today! A __________ of you may want to repair your sails instead. The Coast Guard will be on alert to __________ any sailors in distress.

So, stay tuned and __________ the __________ tomorrow to see if you and your __________ can sail the deep __________ sea in the near future. This is Sailor Sam, in my __________ sailor __________, signing off.

Now it's your turn to come up with your own words with these spelling patterns. Write one more word on each line. You may use your spelling book or dictionary if you get stuck.

oo	*ew*	*ui*	*ue*	*iew*
choose	news	cruising	rescue	view
smooth	crew	suit	true	______
______	few	______	blue	
	blew	______	continue	
	new		______	

Name______________________________

Boning Up On Spelling!

Write your spelling words on the blanks provided. Then complete _____ of the following activities:

- **Spotlight It** List all the smaller words that you see within each spelling word. (For example: *spotlight—spot, light, pot, o,* and *I*.)
- **Howl About It** Use ten of your spelling words to describe yesterday.
- **Bulletin—Dognapper On The Loose** The ransom note says, "Provide one rhyming word for each spelling word."
- **Call Me Speedy** See how fast you can correctly spell each word aloud.
- **Hot Diggity Dog** Write each word expressively. Use shapes and sizes of letters to express the word's meaning.
- **Spot It** Color the bone beside each spelling word you find in a book, magazine, or newspaper.
- **A Spot Test** Write some of the letters of each spelling word. Later complete the word list from your letter clues. Fill in all of the missing letters.
- **Bite-Sized Bits** Copy each spelling word onto a bone pattern. Cut each bone into bite-sized pieces. Mix up the pieces. Then put them back together.
- **A Real Boner** List your spelling words in reverse alphabetical order.
- **Bite Into This** Order your spelling words into a secret pattern. Have your parent guess what the pattern is.
- **Dog-Ear It** Make a spelling dictionary. Label the pages with the letters of the alphabet. Dog-ear the pages with the most difficult words. Study these words throughout the year.

At Home: Fill in a number in the blank above. Each week, have your child complete several different activities using his weekly spelling list.

1. ____________________
2. ____________________
3. ____________________
4. ____________________
5. ____________________
6. ____________________
7. ____________________
8. ____________________
9. ____________________
10. ____________________
11. ____________________
12. ____________________
13. ____________________
14. ____________________
15. ____________________
16. ____________________

Name____ Spelling: *ou*, *oy*, *oi*

Oh Boy, What a Game!

Picture this: The bases are loaded and the score is tied at the bottom of the ninth inning! The home team needs to hit a home run to win.

You are the radio announcer. Use as many words as you can that contain *ou*, *oy*, and *oi*, from the Word Bank as well as your own, to tell what happens next. Underline those words when you have finished.

Winning
Word Bank
noise
out
enjoy
boy
shout
choice
destroy
count
about
soil
scout
stout
aloud
ground
loyal

Name ______________________________

Can You Kick?

Kenny Kincaid likes to play kickball, but needs your help getting some of the neighborhood kids together. He has decided to post an ad in the park. Help Kenny write an ad asking for players to form a new kickball team. Use as many words from the Word Bank as possible.

Rule: The *k* and *ck* in *kick* make the hard *k* sound. Many words that start with *c* also make a hard *k* sound, as in *cookie.*

Now, underline the words you used in your ad.

Word Bank

park, kick, can, cool, come, back, kids, kind, stuck, lucky, keep, lack, stick, neck, deck, count, call, cost, coach, catch

Name______________________________ Spelling: using *s, j, ge, kn, ph*

A Strange Story

The strange story below contains the true tale of a tragic incident that happened in 1986. Read the paragraph carefully. Then circle all the misspelled words and write them correctly in the blanks provided. Some words are not spelled like they sound! Use a dictionary if necessary.

A stranj event happened on the evening of August 26, 1986. About 1,700 people of all ajes died in the valley below Lake Nyos in northwestern Cameroon. When the news spread, scientists arrived from around the world. They new there had to be some explanation. After researching the area, they discovered that the crater lake inside a dormant volcano had filled with carbon dioxide gas. The gas had bubbled out of the lake suddenly and killed knearly every living being in the valley. As sad as it was, at least there was an explanation for this trajedy. Now, know one else would get hurt, just as long as they lived on the far edjes of the valley.

1. ____________ 2. ____________ 3. ____________ 4. ____________

5. ____________ 6. ____________ 7. ____________

Name____ Spelling: *ur, ir, er, or, ear*

Bigfoot Broadcast

Read the following passage and picture an encounter with Bigfoot.

You can call him Bigfoot, Susquatch, or Skunk Ape. Tales of this large, hairy beast have thrilled people for decades. Sightings have been reported in remote areas of North America. Those who have encountered the creature describe it as up to eight feet tall, walking upright on two legs, weighing from three to five hundred pounds and covered in thick, brown hair.

Over the years, several thousand people have reported signs of Bigfoot. Huge footprints have been found in forests. He (or she) has even been captured on film! Imagine strolling in the woods a few feet from your campsite. Suddenly a hairy beast the size of a big car crosses your path! Hairy, smelly (they dont call him Skunk Ape for nothing), and rippling with muscle, Bigfoot lopes off into the forest. Do you follow him? Or do you run in the opposite direction?

Pretend you are a TV reporter who has just witnessed this mysterious beast LIVE! Write a broadcast. Use as many words from the Bigfoot Word Bank as possible.

Bigfoot Word Bank:
early, heard, word, learn, world, prefer, disturb, curious, dirty, furry, earth, search, lurking, worry, scurry, stir, bury, hurry, hurt, certain

Try This: On a sheet of drawing paper, illustrate what might have happened during your up-close sighting, or create a Bigfoot footprint to use in your broadcast.

Peter Piper Picked a Peck of Plurals

Help Peter Piper round up all the plural words he can find. Read each word on the clipboard. Next, write the plural for each noun on the bucket. Use the rules in the box to help you decide how to make each singular word into a plural.

Rules:

1. When a singular noun ends in *s, sh, ch,* or *x,* add *-es.*
2. When a singular noun ends in a consonant and *y,* change the *y* to *i* and add *-es.*
3. If a singular noun ends in *y* with a vowel before it, add *-s.*

A plural noun names more than one person, place, or thing. Plural nouns usually have an *-s* ending.

bench
bush
donkey
country
watch
family
valley
beach
dessert
daisy
glass
rose
box
pebble
tiger

Opera Night

Sally's parents had an eventful evening when they went out for Opera Night. Sally wrote this story about it, but needs help with her plurals. Help Sally by changing the **bold** words from singular to plural. Write the plural of each bold word in a blank.

Mom and Dad had been looking forward to going to the opera for weeks. Finally, the big night arrived. Mom dressed up in a long, gold evening gown, and Dad put on his tux. As they were getting ready, Mom asked Dad to take two **loaf** of bread out of the oven. Dad donned the oven mitts, opened the oven, and placed the **loaf** on two **shelf** to cool. "Mmmm. What a wonderful smell!" he thought to himself. He decided they would treat **themself** to homemade bread and jam when they returned. In anticipation, he put two **knife** and two plates on the table.

It was a cool autumn night, and the **leaf** were falling from the trees. On the way out, Mom grabbed her **glove** and their wool **scarf**. They locked the door and set the alarm to prevent **thief** from getting in. As they pulled out of the driveway, Mom noticed that the geese were flying south and two **wolf** were howling at the full moon, but Dad was still thinking about warm bread.

On the way to the opera house, Mom and Dad picked up two friends and their **wife**. When the couples arrived at the opera, they had a wonderful time, but Dad was still thinking about warm bread. Throughout the performance, he couldn't wait to get home to devour a whole loaf!

Arriving home, Mom and Dad went directly into the kitchen, not knowing they were in for the surprise of their **life**. Entering the kitchen, they discovered that the two **loaf** were gone without a trace. Not even crumbs were found at the scene. Just then, the two robbers ran out from behind the kitchen door. The two **thief** were Beau and Baby, our basset hounds!

______________________ ______________________

______________________ ______________________

______________________ ______________________

______________________ ______________________

______________________ ______________________

______________________ ______________________

Name ____________________

Flights of Fancy

Read the passage. Circle all of the plural nouns. If the boldfaced words are incorrect, rewrite them below the balloon.

Hint: Some singular nouns don't become plural in the usual way. There is no set rule for these irregular plurals, so you must memorize them. Below are a few examples:

Singular	Plural
woman	women
trousers	trousers
ox	oxen
mouse	mice
deer	deer

Our hot-air balloon adventure began early in the morning. We jumped out of bed at 4:00 AM when the alarm went off. We wanted plenty of time to drive to the farm and meet with our flight instructor and crew. Takeoff was scheduled for sunrise. It was chilly, so we dressed in **pants** and jackets. As the sun came up, the beautiful balloon was inflated, and we were ready to go. We anxiously climbed into the gondola. In addition to the pilot, there were two **woman** and two **child** on board. The pilot gave the signal, and the **people** on the ground let go of the ropes.

As the balloon lifted higher and higher, I could see the roof of the barn and two **ox** standing nearby. I think I even saw two **mouse** running toward the barn. We floated silently above the large farm, passing over a field where **sheep** were grazing. As we climbed over the mountain, we spotted several **deer** and **elk** in a meadow below. When we drifted toward a lake, I saw ducks in the marshes and two **moose** in the distance.

We felt like we were walking in the clouds. The rest of the world was just over the horizon. But, like all good things, our journey had to end. We landed beside the lake where our spotter crew and a gaggle of **goose** greeted us. What a great day! It was good to have our **foot** on the ground.

__________ __________

__________ __________

__________ __________

Name ____________________ Spelling: plural noun review

Packaged Plurals

Preston Peabody is positively puzzled! He knows that a plural noun names more than one person, place, or thing. But sometimes he gets the rules mixed up. One of the nouns he placed in each gift box below does not fit the same rule as the others.

Directions: Use the information on the gift tag to identify the rule for the nouns listed on each box. First write the rule number on the ribbon at the top of each box. Then write the plural form of each noun on the blank provided. Finally circle the noun that does not fit the rule in each box.

Rules For Forming Plural Nouns

1. Add *s* to form the plural of most nouns. **Example:** girl—girls
2. Add *es* to nouns that end in the letters *ch, sh, s, x,* or *z.* **Example:** church—churches
3. Add *es* to nouns that end with a *consonant* before an *o.* **Example:** hero—heroes
4. For nouns that end with a *consonant* before a *y,* change the *y* to an *i* and add *es.* **Example:** puppy—puppies
5. For nouns that end with a *vowel* before a *y,* just add *s.* **Example:** monkey—monkeys
6. For nouns that end in *f* or *fe,* change the ending to *ve* and add *s.* **Example:** leaf—leaves
7. For some nouns, use the same singular and plural forms. **Example:** deer—deer
8. For some nouns, change the spelling of the singular noun. **Example:** man—men

1. zero ________
2. zoo ________
3. potato ________
4. tomato ________
5. hero ________

1. knife ________
2. tooth ________
3. thief ________
4. wife ________
5. shelf ________

1. suitcase ________
2. rock ________
3. flower ________
4. egg ________
5. sandwich ________

1. donkey ________
2. strawberry ________
3. daisy ________
4. butterfly ________
5. candy ________

1. saleswoman ________
2. grandchild ________
3. ox ________
4. foot ________
5. hand ________

1. box ________
2. lunch ________
3. goose ________
4. dish ________
5. kiss ________

1. turkey ________
2. donkey ________
3. key ________
4. birthday ________
5. library ________

1. moose ________
2. elk ________
3. sheep ________
4. mouse ________
5. deer ________

 Name________________________________

Easy Does It at the Zoo

There is a lot to see on a trip to the zoo! Everyone has a favorite animal. Which monkey is funnier? Which animal is biggest? In the sentences below, underline the correct form of the adjective that best fits the sentence. Use the rules in the rule box to help you.

1. That giant gorilla is (meaner, meanest) than his father.
2. The large lion in the back is the (louder, loudest) of all the lions in the zoo.
3. The playful monkey in the middle is the (cuter, cutest) monkey of the bunch.
4. The laughing hyena was the (funnier, funniest) animal that we saw today.
5. My favorite animals are the giraffes. They are the (cooler, coolest) animals of all.
6. On the way home, I fell asleep (faster, fastest) than my friend Tommy.

Rules

1. Add *-er* to an adjective when you compare two people, places, or things.
2. Add *-est* to an adjective when you compare three or more people, places, or things.
3. When an adjective ends in a single consonant following a single vowel, double the consonant and add *-er* or *-est.*

Now, turn the following words into adjectives that compare. Then use each word with *-est* in a sentence. The first one has been done for you.

1. big	bigger	biggest
2. hot	______	______
3. thin	______	______
4. flat	______	______
5. red	______	______
6. fat	______	______

7. The elephant was the biggest animal in the zoo.
8. ______________________________
   ______________________________.
9. ______________________________
   ______________________________.
10. ______________________________
    ______________________________.
11. ______________________________
    ______________________________.
12. ______________________________
    ______________________________.

Name____

Look Out for Sloppy Spelling!

Read each sentence below. Underline each misspelled word and write the correct spelling in the space provided.
Hint: There are enough blanks for each mistake!

1. Several woman went shopping for shooz and spent hundreds of dollars.

   ______________, ______________, ______________

2. My cousen is a real beuty. Her heit is five feet eight inches, and she has long blonde hair and a hart of gold.

   ______________, ______________, ______________, ______________

3. My uncle played the lottery twentie times and finally one a millian dollars.

   ______________, ______________, ______________

4. The concert I attended was filled with fordy thousend yung peopel.

   ______________, ______________, ______________, ______________

5. We went to an iland that was thirdy-three miles away. It was in the middle of a beutiful blue oshen.

   ______________, ______________, ______________, ______________

6. Someone left this chocolate brownie. Do you know whos desert this is?

   ______________, ______________

7. Arithmatic is my favorite subject. I love to work with desimals and all kinds of numarels. Do you?

   ______________, ______________, ______________

8. I shure like math and multiplying three-diget numbers. What is your favorite subject?

   ______________, ______________

9. I often help my brother anser social studies questons, so he doesn't have to gess. Whom do *you* help?

   ______________, ______________, ______________

10. I love suger cookies. I could eat eghteen or ninteen of them. How about you?

    ______________, ______________, ______________

Puzzled by Spelling?

Solve the puzzle of some commonly misspelled words with the following activity. Read the word in each puzzle piece below. If the word is spelled correctly, color the piece yellow. If the word is not spelled correctly, color the piece blue.

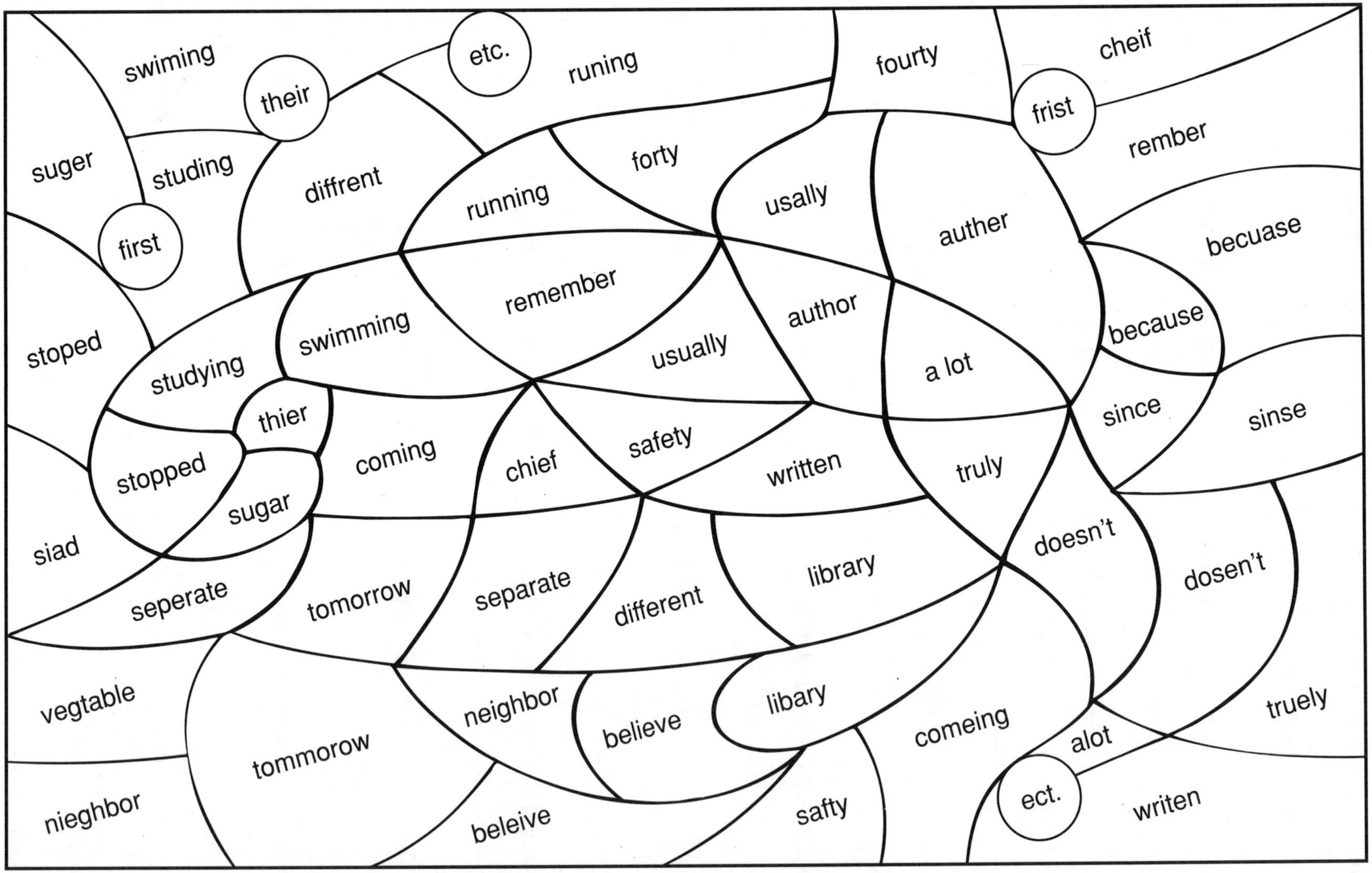

Try This: Can you spell three different words with the letters *a, e, l, r,* and *y?*

Fourth-Grade Parent Page

Vocabulary Development and Dictionary Skills

Fourth graders write stories, personal narratives, comparisons, contrasts, letters, and descriptive passages. To achieve these literary feats, fourth graders must use their word-analysis skills to increase their written vocabulary. Fourth-grade teachers encourage vocabulary development in a number of ways, most notably with weekly vocabulary lessons that involve reading, writing, and testing. Weekly word lists often include words from the reading, science, social studies, or math topics being studied.

Word analysis begins with basic *root words,* such as the word *act.* Fourth graders quickly learn they can build new words—such as *action, react,* and *reaction*—by adding *prefixes* and *suffixes.*

Your fourth grader will build on her word base by

- using knowledge of letter-sound combinations and syllables
- using knowledge of root words, prefixes, and suffixes
- locating meaning, pronunciation, and derivations in a dictionary, a glossary, or other sources
- using knowledge of word origins, derivations, synonyms, antonyms, and idioms to determine meaning of unfamiliar words
- determining the meaning of unfamiliar words
- recognizing words with multiple meanings
- reading for comprehension in every subject area
- interpreting *figurative language,* such as similes and metaphors

To further your child's vocabulary development, try the ideas on the next page and the Try This activities on the pages that follow.

21/22

Synonym Scramble

Use your child's weekly vocabulary list to play Synonym Scramble. First, identify together the vocabulary words most easily linked to synonyms. (This will be easy in fourth grade, as most words are common ones.) Next, each of you will come up with a list of as many synonyms for each word as possible. Finally, come together and combine your lists, crossing off any duplicates. Your child can keep each list of synonyms to use as a word bank for future writing assignments.

Twisting Tongues

Children love tongue twisters, so why not build on that love of language fun? Each week, go over your student's graded vocabulary test or worksheets. Next, have your child write a tongue twister for each word, being careful to only use twisting words that help define or explain the word. Try this tongue-twister task each week—the challenge is forever fun and unique!

Word-a-Day

Encourage family participation in a Word-a-Day program. Invest in a personal dictionary for each child, be it paperback, large-print, or many volumes. Provide colorful index cards and bold markers. Each member of the family, beginning with your fourth grader, can randomly select a word from the dictionary, write it in marker on an index card, and post it in a place where it can be seen throughout the day, such as the refrigerator or bathroom mirror. Keep up with this idea each day, and the whole family could increase its vocabulary!

Word Search

Use the family refrigerator to display new vocabulary words. Post a blank piece of paper labeled "Word List" in a place of prominence. Then encourage family members, but most especially your fourth grader, to place words on the fridge that he may not understand, such as those heard on TV, found in the morning paper, or spoken by other family members. At the end of each week, have your child look up that week's words in the dictionary. This will shortly become a habit that is hard to break, and one that could just last a lifetime.

Get Cross (Words)!

Crossword puzzle books are a fun and educational way of building your child's vocabulary. Invest in a crossword book on your child's developmental level, as well as a crossword dictionary for him. To make him feel like a special word detective, label the cover with your child's name and write an encouraging inscription inside. Next, encourage your child to complete the crossword puzzles, choosing to tackle one or more per week. Invest in your own crossword book and dictionary, and spend time completing these puzzles together!

Name ______________________________

Less of Loch *Ness*

Want to solve an ancient mystery? Here's your chance!
Read the following passage.
Then circle all of the words that end in the suffix *-ness* or *-less.*

For many years, people have said there's a large dinosaur-like monster living in Loch Ness in Scotland. Throughout the last 100 years, an endless series of sightings of a monster in the deep lake has been reported. Like the mysterious Bigfoot creature, the existence of the Loch Ness monster, better known as Nessie, has sometimes been supported by fuzzy photo images. The truthfulness of this evidence is disputed.

Nessie is usually seen swimming in the darkness. Although a dinosaur of her size would be very heavy, the water makes her seem weightless. No one knows for sure if she exists. Those who think they have seen her sometimes feel hopeless because of the lack of real evidence. Needless to say, they may only find happiness when they finally encounter Nessie face to face or, at least, get others to agree that Nessie exists.

Now answer the following questions:

1. List all seven words that end in *-ness* or *-less:* ______________________________

____

2. Do you think Nessie exists? Explain why or why not, using as many words that end in *-ness* or *-less* as possible. ______________________________

____

____

Name ____________________ Suffixes: *-ly*, *-ful*, *-ment*

Haunted Happenings

What would you do if a **seemingly** harmless business deal turned haunted?
Read the following *poltergeist* paragraph.
Then add the suffix *-ly*, *-ful* or *-ment* to each bold word.
Write the corrected words in the blanks.

When my neighbor, Mr. Poltergeist, had to leave town **unexpected** on business, he asked my friend Becky and me to take turns walking his dog, Boo. We decided **agreeable** that each of us would walk Boo once a day. There was just one problem with this **agree**. The first time I went to Mr. Poltergeist's house, I spotted a sign and gasped in **astonish**. The sign on the front door said, "Beware of the dog!" I don't scare **easy**, but I was **definite** **fear** to open the door alone. I called Becky and told her the situation **nervous.** We decided to walk Boo together, and I **secret** breathed a sigh of relief.

Later that day, Becky and I arrived at the house prepared to win Boo's friendship with dog biscuits. We wore our running shoes just in case. After finding the hidden key, we opened the door **hopeful**. We were greeted **eager** by a big black Lab. We **quick** placed the leash on Boo, and he bounded **happy** down the street. He was quite a **play** dog. **Lucky** we had a strong leash. It was an **achieve** just to hang on as he pulled us **powerful** down the street. There was no way to run **graceful**. After several blocks, we were **total** exhausted. **Final**, we brought Boo back home, **thank** to be alive. We opened the door **quiet** and looked inside **careful**. We saw **sudden** to our **amaze** that the house was **hopeless** haunted!

Try This: What happened to our two heroes next? Finish the story using as many words as possible containing the suffixes *-ly*, *-ful*, and *-ment*. Underline those words when you finish!

Name ____

Occupational Hazards

Confused Claude always has a little trouble deciding whether to add *-er* or *-or* to words that name someone who performs a certain occupation or task. Help him by spelling each occupation.

Directions: Add the suffix *-er* or *-or* to the following base words. You may have to drop the *e* or *y* before adding the *-er* to some of the words.

teach ____________	drive ____________
count ____________	preach ____________
skate ____________	design ____________
visit ____________	counsel ____________

Use the same suffixes to write a new word for each underlined word below. The first one is done for you.

One who can teach: teacher

1. one who sings ____________
2. one who reads ____________
3. one who paints ____________
4. one who counts ____________
5. one who acts ____________
6. one who helps ____________
7. one who builds ____________
8. one who can take a photograph ____________
9. one who can write ____________
10. one who can write a biography ____________

Name____

Dangling Suffixes

Read the paragraph below. Then reread it again, circling words that end with the suffixes *-ful*, *-less*, and *-ing*. These endings change the base word. Write those words at the bottom of the page.

There are many types of jellyfish, but one of the deadliest is the sea wasp, or marine stinger. The body of this box-type jelly can get as big as a basketball, with up to 60 tentacles hanging down as long as 15 feet! These jellyfish are not aggressive though. They don't have to be. They swim up to five miles per hour—pretty quickly for a jellyfish—dangling their long tentacles in the surf behind them. Then something, usually a fish, gets caught up in their tentacles.

The tentacles of a jellyfish are practically invisible. This is where the stinging cells, called *nematocysts,* are located. The poison in these cells kills their prey almost instantly. This prevents the helpless victim from struggling and thrashing the jelly's delicate tissue. Since the prey is now defenseless, the jelly can take its time devouring its meal. The tentacles are quite helpful for the jellies, but quite deadly for those who get tangled in their "webs."

______________ ______________ ______________

______________ ______________ ______________

______________ ______________ ______________

Try This: Can you find words with these suffixes: *-est, -ive, -ly?*

Name ____

Creature Feature

Have you ever wanted to direct a movie? Well, here's your chance! (Sort of.)
Read the paragraph below.
Underline the words that end in the suffix *-tion* or *-ure.*
Can you find all 22 words? Write each word on the lines.

Steven Spielberg has always had a great imagination. As a child, he would rearrange the furniture and pretend to be on a movie set. As he grew older, his family told him to grow up! Luckily, he never really did. He continues to use his imagination to make motion pictures.

Spielberg has made many amazing feature films. Have you seen *ET, Raiders of the Lost Ark, Jurassic Park,* and *Back to the Future?* In each of his action movies, Spielberg pays attention to details. Before shooting, he is on a mission to choose the best location. He may look at many places in many nations.

In addition, Spielberg has to think about weather conditions and nature. Heavy rains will stop production. Muddy roads and thick jungles cause problems with transportation. Wild animals and pesky insects are trouble! Special-effects experts plan carefully for stunts. These crews must use extra caution on the set. Actors and stuntmen get careful instructions on what to do and when to do it. A new movie sensation takes shape under Spielberg's direction! Who knows what creatures Spielberg will feature in his next adventure?

Now, use your own imagination! Think of your favorite movie. Create a movie poster to describe your awesome movie. Use as many words that end in *-tion* and *-ure* as possible.

____________________ ____________________
____________________ ____________________
____________________ ____________________
____________________ ____________________
____________________ ____________________
____________________ ____________________
____________________ ____________________
____________________ ____________________
____________________ ____________________
____________________ ____________________
____________________ ____________________

Name ____

Puzzling Prefixes

Puzzled Pete has a rough time deciding between the prefixes *un-*, *dis-*, *ex-*, *de-*, and *re-*. Read the following sentences. Then underline the words that contain the prefixes that are so puzzling to Pete!

Hint: A prefix is a letter or group of letters added to the beginning of a base word. A prefix changes the meaning of a word.

1. We were in a state of disbelief when the magician made the woman vanish into thin air.
2. We were unable to get the safe open.
3. After the mission, the pilot had to debrief the colonel.
4. He had to repay the loan with interest.
5. Explain the report so everyone can understand it.

Now add one of the prefixes from above to each word in the parentheses to complete the following sentences.

6. No one could decide which car was the safest. They all seemed to __________. (agree)
7. __________ your steps to see where you left your keys. (trace)
8. She is very sweet. She never has an __________ word to say about anyone. (kind)
9. I heard her __________ from the back of the room that she knew the answer. (claim)
10. The exterminator needed to __________ the whole house when the back door was left open for a week. (bug)
11. He had to __________ the pair of shoes for one that fit. (change)
12. It's hard to __________ a bad habit that you have had for a long time. (do)

Name________________________________

Searching for Suffixes and Prefixes in Space

Circle the words with the prefixes and suffixes *re-*, *de-*, *dis-*, *un-*, and *-ly* floating by in outer space. Then use the circled words to fill in the Mission Accomplished chart below. (The first one is done for you.)

Hint: Remember, sometimes the spelling of a root word changes when an ending is added.

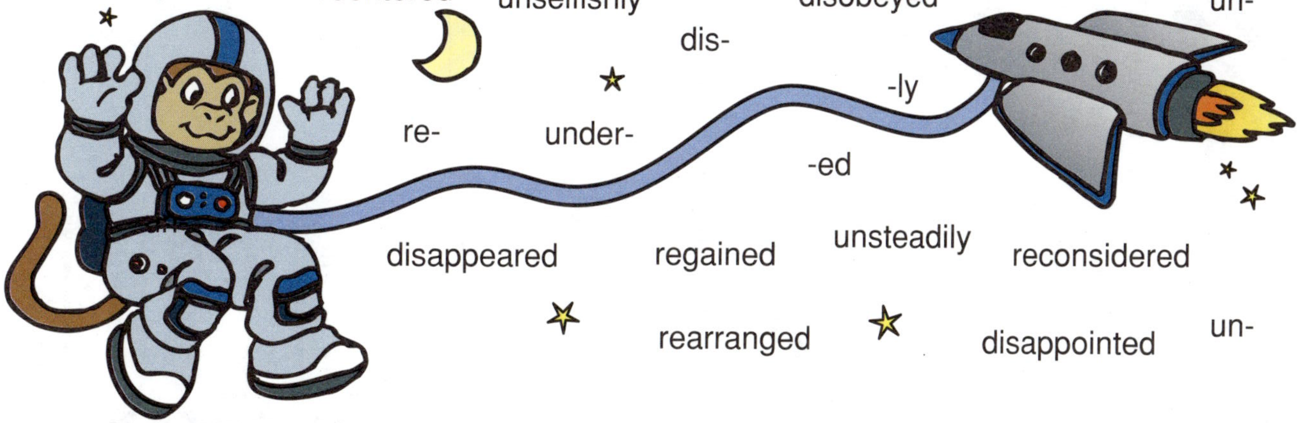

unconcerned reentered unselfishly disobeyed un-

dis- -ly

re- under- -ed

disappeared regained unsteadily reconsidered

rearranged disappointed un-

Circled Word	Root Word	Prefix	Suffix
disappeared	appear	dis-	-ed
____________	____________	____________	____________
____________	____________	____________	____________
____________	____________	____________	____________
____________	____________	____________	____________
____________	____________	____________	____________
____________	____________	____________	____________
____________	____________	____________	____________
____________	____________	____________	____________
____________	____________	____________	____________
____________	____________	____________	____________

How many words can you think of that have a suffix and a prefix? Think for a minute, and then list as many as you can in five minutes. Set your timer and begin. Good luck!

____________ ____________
____________ ____________
____________ ____________
____________ ____________
____________ ____________
____________ ____________
____________ ____________
____________ ____________
____________ ____________
____________ ____________
____________ ____________
____________ ____________
____________ ____________

Name____

Compound Chain

The more links in a chain, the stronger it becomes. Sometimes words are like chains, too. In fact, compound words are formed when two smaller words are put together, or combined.

Directions: Write the two words that make up each of the compound words below:

1. blueberry ______________ ______________
2. cornbread ______________ ______________
3. airstrip ______________ ______________
4. sunlight ______________ ______________
5. snowman ______________ ______________

Look at the following words within each piece of the chain. Draw a line matching the words that make up a compound word, and then write them in the blanks provided.

news	burst	______________
sail	fall	______________
rain	bird	______________
blue	boat	______________
flash	worm	______________
cloud	paper	______________
silk	light	______________
story	book	______________

Name____________________

The Riches Of King Tut's Tomb

Dr. Howard Carter gazed spellbound through the doorway. He saw armloads of riches. Six hard years of digging led to this great discovery. He would wire Lord Carnarvon with the good news. Carnarvon, a British nobleman, had paid for Carter's trip.

Carter had discovered the underground tomb of an Egyptian king. The tomb dated back to 1300 B.C. It was the first Egyptian tomb found undamaged. Grave robbers had not taken anything. Footstools, chairs, jewels, necklaces, earrings, and other riches filled Carter's view. Nearby were the king's chariots, his hunting bow, and even his sandals. Ancient Egyptians were always buried with their favorite belongings.

News of Carter's 1922 discovery was broadcast on radio stations. Newspaper headlines captured the interest of people everywhere. Years later King Tutankhamen's tomb still remains the most well-known archaeological find in history.

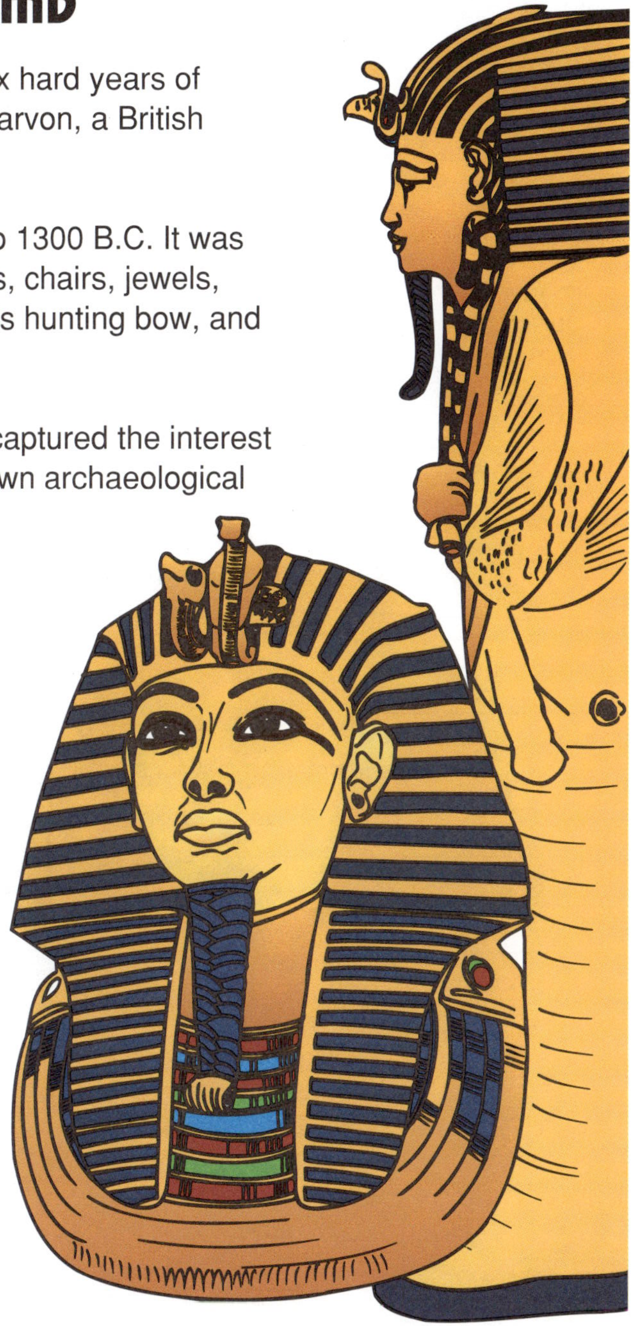

A. Build Word Skills Circle each compound word in the story.

B. Expand Your Vocabulary Find two words in each sentence below that you can turn into a compound word. Write the word in the blank provided.

1. They are keeping the Egyptians' relics in a safe place. ____________
2. Walk this way to view the mummy. ____________
3. Dr. Carter wrote a note about his findings in his book. ____________
4. The body of Tutankhamen had some decay. ____________
5. A collar shaped like a wreath was placed on the mummy. ____________
6. Egyptians believed in a life after death. ____________
7. Burial tombs were built under the ground for pharaohs. ____________

The Great Wall Of China

At one time, China had many rul**ers**. These rulers often put up walls to protect their lands. About 2,200 years ago, one ruler unit**ed** the different kingdoms. The new emperor began connect**ing** some of the walls. He wanted to protect China's northern borders from the Huns. The Huns were a nomad**ic** group who had no real homes. They attacked on horseback using short, power**ful** bows. Chinese farmers great**ly** feared these warri**ors**.

Emperor Shi Huangdi ordered his subjects to build a continu**ous** wall across northern China. A million manu**al** laborers worked on the wall. Those who complained or ran away were caught and often buried in the wall. After ten length**y** years, the 3,750-mile wall was complete. It was made of dirt, stones, and bricks. A stone roadway ran along the top. Watchtowers and gatehouses were placed along the wall as lookout posts. The wall provided protect**ion** for China's northern borders for more than a thousand years. Sections of the Great Wall now lie in ruins. Yet it remains the larg**est** man-made structure in the world.

A. Build Word Skills Match the vocabulary word (with a boldface suffix) from the story with its meaning below.

1. past tense of *unite* ____________
2. in a great manner ____________
3. an act or process of joining ____________
4. biggest ____________
5. full of power ____________
6. quality of being unbroken ____________
7. relating to the hands ____________
8. inclined to be long ____________
9. state of being protected ____________
10. one who makes war ____________
11. one who rules ____________
12. relating to nomads ____________

B. Expand Your Vocabulary List the 12 suffixes from the words in Part A. Beside each suffix, write two more words that each have the same suffix.

Name______________________________

The Mystery Of Stonehenge

Outside Salisbury, England, stands an **un**usual monument. It is called Stonehenge. This **uni**que group of stones is one of the few things **pre**historic people built that is still standing.

A ditch circled the outer **peri**meter of Stonehenge. Within it, huge single stones called **mono**liths formed a large circle. Smaller blocks stood on top of them. Within this circle was an inner circle of blue stones. It **en**closed two groups of **tri**lithons. A trilithon was a group of three stones. Two of the stones stood upright and another one joined them across the top. At the very center of Stonehenge was a single stone. It is known as the Altar Stone.

Why was Stonehenge built? Gerald Hawkins, an astronomer who studied Stonehenge, believes the stones were used as a calendar. He used a computer to help him prove his theory. Hawkins showed how the layout of the stones **fore**told eclipses and equinoxes. Is this true? If so, it would **dis**credit those who believe prehistoric people weren't very smart.

A. Build Word Skills Match each boldface prefix in the story with its meaning below.

1. before ____________
2. one ____________
3. occurring earlier ____________
4. three ____________
5. single, one ____________
6. not ____________
7. around, near, about ____________
8. in ____________
9. not ____________

B. Expand Your Vocabulary Match each prefix with its meaning shown on the right.

1. *Uncle Tom's Cabin* was an **anti**slavery novel.
2. Maria and Jonathan sang a **du**et.
3. The rails of a railroad track are **para**llel to each other.
4. The candidate is a **pro**ponent of civil rights.
5. **Re**read the directions.
6. Be sure to **in**clude Bo in your group.
7. Please **re**mit your payment on time.
8. Jesse **trans**ferred to a new school.

Meanings:
beside
back
again
across, over
in favor of
against
two
into

The Beauty Of The Taj Mahal

India's Taj Mahal is one of the most beautiful monuments in the world. **Sci**entists marvel at the perfect **sym**metry of the building. Each half is a mirror image of the other. It was built in the 17th century by an Indian emperor named Shah Jahan. This gleaming white marble tomb rises 76 **meter**s high. Seen from afar it looks like a priceless jewel. It was built as a tomb for the Shah's most beloved wife. *Taj Mahal* is short for his wife's title, which meant "Crown of the Palace."

It took more than 20,000 workers 20 years to build the majestic Taj Mahal. It stands within an attractive walled garden. A large pond is located in front of the tomb. It reflects the minarets (towers) and dome of the building. Islamic calli**gra**-**ph**y covers the palatial walls. The Shah hoped the beauty of the Taj Mahal would in**spir**e people everywhere to strive for perfection.

A. Build Word Skills Below are the base words of 12 words used in the story. Match a word from the story to its base word.

1. Islam ____________
2. far ____________
3. gleam ____________
4. empire ____________
5. price ____________
6. palace ____________
7. attract ____________
8. love ____________
9. beauty ____________
10. perfect ____________
11. majesty ____________
12. science ____________

B. Expand Your Vocabulary Match each meaning below with its boldface word root in the story. Then write one other word that has the same root.

meaning	word root	another example
1. with; along with; together	______	______
2. measure	______	______
3. breath, live	______	______
4. know	______	______
5. write	______	______

Name ________________________

The Faces Of Mount Rushmore

Gutzon Borglum gazed up at the **magn**ificent 60-foot-tall faces carved into granite. They were faces of the presidents he admired most: George Washington, Thomas Jefferson, Abraham Lincoln, and Theodore Roosevelt. Only the final touches needed to be done now. More than 400 people had worked on this demanding task. Many were skilled miners. **Dynam**ite was used to remove and shape much of the rock. Borglum and his son Lincoln had supervised each step. It took 14 years to complete this in**cred**ible job!

Borglum thought of the **num**erous problems he had overcome. **Nat**ive Americans in South Dakota opposed the **mem**orial. They did not want a monument carved into the sacred Black Hills. **Leg**islation was slow to fund the project. There were also **geo**logical problems—a **fract**ure had occurred in Thomas Jefferson's face.

Viewing the **fin**ished monument, Borglum knew it had all been worth it.

A. Build Word Skills Match each boldface root in the story with its definition below. If you're unsure, use a dictionary.

1. power ____________
2. end ____________
3. earth ____________
4. break ____________
5. believe ____________
6. remember ____________
7. law ____________
8. great ____________
9. to be born ____________
10. number ____________

B. Expand Your Vocabulary Circle the root in each word below. Use the root's meaning to help you write a short definition of the word. Use a dictionary if you need help.

1. enumerate ____________
2. magnify ____________
3. legal ____________
4. geography ____________
5. dynamo ____________
6. fraction ____________
7. credible ____________
8. final ____________
9. nativity ____________
10. memo ____________

Name______________________________

Synonym Sweets

Hop on over to the bookshelf and get a dictionary to use for this synonym challenge! Each word below has a matching *synonym*—a word with the same meaning—that can be found on a jelly bean in the jar. Write the correct synonym on the line. Then color the matching jelly bean. When all the synonyms have been found, there should be two uncolored jelly beans that are antonyms in your jar.

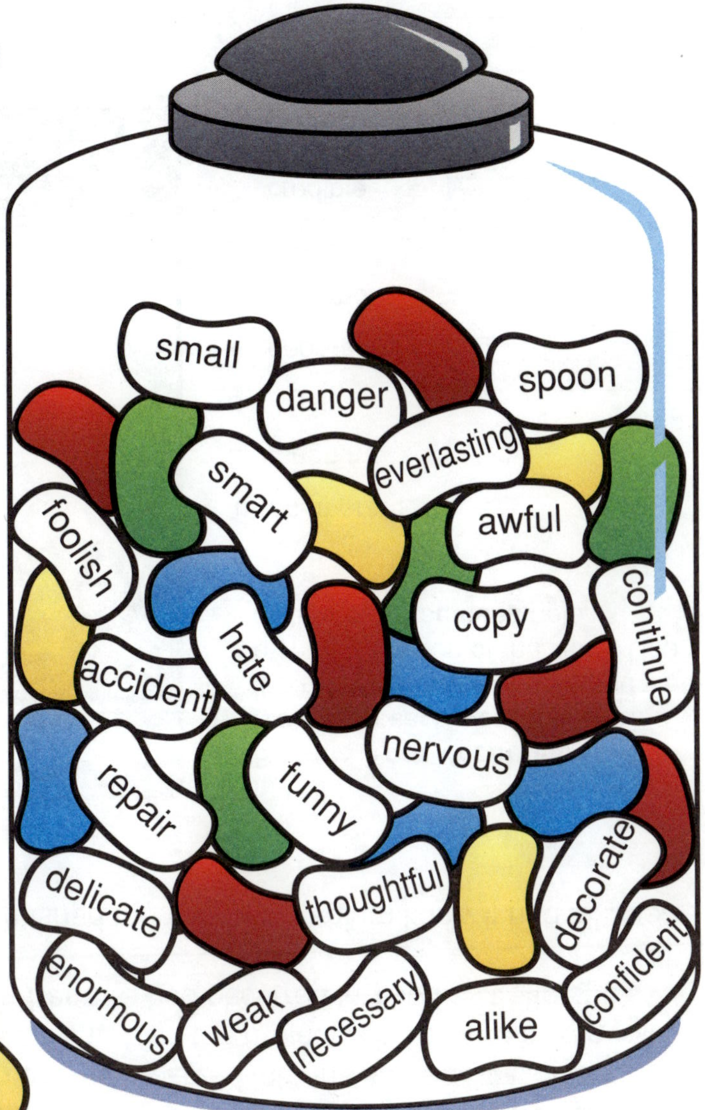

1. minute ____________
2. bright ____________
3. loathe ____________
4. mishap ____________
5. similar ____________
6. dreadful ____________
7. frivolous ____________
8. colossal ____________
9. endure ____________
10. embellish ____________
11. fragile ____________
12. feeble ____________
13. comical ____________
14. ladle ____________
15. imitate ____________
16. essential ____________
17. perpetual ____________
18. mend ____________
19. jeopardy ____________
20. considerate ____________

Try This: Choose any five of the words listed above and write an antonym for each one. Remember that an *antonym* is a word with an opposite meaning.

Name ____

Star-Spangled Synonyms

What if Francis Scott Key had used different words in the poem that became our national anthem? On the lines provided, write at least one synonym for each boldfaced word in the anthem below. Use a dictionary or a thesaurus if you need help.

Words by
Francis Scott Key
(1779–1843)

The Star-Spangled Banner

Music by
J. Stafford Smith
(1750–1836)

Oh— say can you see, by the dawn's ear - ly light, what so proud - ly we
hail'd at the twi - light's last gleam - ing? Whose broad stripes and bright stars through the
per - il - ous fight, o'er the ram - parts we watched were so gal - lant - ly
stream - ing? And the rock - ets' red glare, the bombs burst - ing in air, gave
proof through the night that our flag was still there. Oh, say does that star - span - gled
ban - ner yet wave O'er the land of the free and the home of the brave?

see: ______________________

broad: ______________________

bright: ______________________

perilous: ______________________

watched: ______________________

glare: ______________________

bursting: ______________________

banner: ______________________

free: ______________________

home: ______________________

Name ____________________

Grandma Moses (1860–1961)

Artist

Anna Mary Moses thought about her life. She had worked hard raising a **large** family and helping her husband on the farm. Now she was a widow. Her children were **grown.** Farm life no longer demanded so much of her time. Why not devote herself to painting? She had **always** thought she would like to pursue her **love** of art. Yes, she would begin painting those picturesque scenes she was so fond of.

At first Anna Mary's work drew little attention. She placed several paintings at a **local** pharmacy. They ranged in price from $3.00 to $5.00. Two years later she had an exhibition at an art gallery in New York City. Her work was gaining attention! She was now 80 years old, and people called her "Grandma Moses."

Grandma Moses completed more than 1,500 pictures before her death at the age of 101. **Many** of her paintings were landscapes and childhood scenes. "Always something pleasing and cheerful; I like **bright** colors and activity," said Mrs. Moses. Her choice of topics explained some of her popularity. Many people liked the feelings of a **simple,** peaceful, happy childhood her scenes evoked.

"What an extraordinary person," many said about this plain-spoken woman from New York. Grandma Moses never had a painting lesson. She used **old** coffee cans to keep her paint. She **rarely** painted on canvas because of its expense. Yet her work was well received by art lovers worldwide.

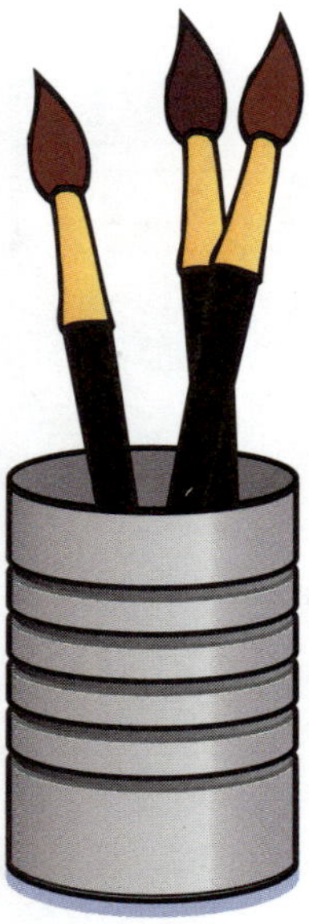

Expand Your Vocabulary

1. Circle each of the following vocabulary words in the selection. Then find the definition in the dictionary.

   picturesque pharmacy exhibition evoked extraordinary

2. Now write each word in a category below. Then give each category a title. Two blanks have been filled for you.

   drugstore, apothecary, ____________ : places where ____________

   exposition, show, *exhibition* : places where ____________

   roused, stirred, ____________ : caused to ____________

   unspoiled, idyllic, ____________ : a state of ____________

   exceptional, unusual, ____________ : a state of *being beyond the ordinary or usual*

3. List each boldface word on another piece of paper. Beside each word, write a word that has an opposite meaning.

Harriet Beecher Stowe (1811–1896)

Author Of *Uncle Tom's Cabin*

My dear sister,

Slavery is so ***abominable!*** *The thought of owning another person leaves such an* ***acrid*** *taste in my mouth. Perhaps my novel will* ***rally*** *Americans against this evil. I've been heartened by the* ***amiable*** *responses that I've already received. However, I fear many in the South will find the* ***book*** *loathsome. Some say it may hasten a war. I* ***abhor*** *war—but better a war than slavery.*

In Christ,
Harriet

Harriet didn't like to see her country torn over the issue of slavery. What could she do? She couldn't preach openly from the pulpit like her famous brother. She was only a housewife with six children. A friend suggested she use her pen. Harriet pondered this idea. It was true she had been writing since she was a small child. She had published a book titled *Primary Geography For Children* and short stories about life in New England. Why not write a novel about the evils of slavery?

Harriet was sitting in church when the idea for her book suddenly came. It was almost like a vision. Harriet couldn't wait to get home and begin. She named the slave "Tom." The master was "Simon Legree." Her story was so vivid that readers couldn't forget it. *Uncle Tom's Cabin* became the biggest best-seller in 19th-century America. It was translated into at least 23 languages. Harriet had written America's first protest novel. And it changed the world!

Opposites Or The Same?

Identify each pair of words as *antonyms* or *synonyms.* Use a dictionary if you are unsure.

1. *rally* and *excite* ____________________
2. *abominable* and *lovely* ____________________
3. *acrid* and *sweet* ____________________
4. *novel* and *book* ____________________
5. *amiable* and *favorable* ____________________
6. *abhor* and *hate* ____________________

Expand Your Vocabulary

Circle the following words in the selection. Find the definition in a dictionary.

loathsome	pulpit
pondered	vision
protest	vivid

Name ______________________________ Homophones

Similar Sounds

Homophones are words that sound the same but have different spellings or meanings. Solve the crossword puzzle below by finding the homophones for some common words.

ACROSS

1. their, they're
2. bear
5. inn
6. rode, rowed
8. buy
10. hear
12. sent, cent
14. to, too
16. for, fore
17. owe
19. meet
21. herd
23. won
24. way
25. seen

DOWN

1. threw
2. by
3. ate
4. hair
7. ant
9. bee
11. write, rite
13. close
15. weight
18. ore
20. I
22. dough

Name ____________________

Watt Dew Ewe No About Columbus?
(What Do You Know About Columbus?)

Directions: *Homophones* are words that sound the same but have different meanings or spellings. Read each sentence below to find one or more homophones that are used incorrectly. Underline each mistake you find. Then write the correct word(s) on the line(s) provided. *Hint: Each sentence's number tells you how many mistakes it has.*

1. Christopher Columbus loved the see.
   ____
2. He would stand in the bough of the boat and watch the waves brake against the ship.
   ____
3. "If we follow this root," he said, "we will bee their soon."
   ____
4. The cabin buoy tolled the captain that sum of the crew were planning a mutiny that knight.
   ____
5. Columbus guest that his sun did knot no those plans were maid.
   ____
6. Columbus faced his men and said, "Chews mutiny oar choose to weight four one more weak. Buy then, we will land or turn back." ____________________
7. Awl threw that chili knight, the wind blue, and the cent of fear was in the heir.
   ____
8. Columbus might have preyed, "Hour sale is torn, and the bottom of the boat has a whole. Maybe this feet was to big four us. Show us the weigh." ____________________
9. Of coarse, spending a lot of thyme on a ship that sighs wood ware down any strong man, but it wood really bee hard four the young boys on bored. ____________________
   ____
10. Write when the crew was about to give up, they saw a bird sore overhead, a fresh branch with flours floating on the tied, and a peace of carved would drifting buy. Every I strained to see a knew land. What a tail to tell their grandchildren! ____________________
   ____

Name ______________________________

Tracking Down Word Meanings

Were these tracks made by a sleuth of bears or a gaggle of geese? Such words as *sleuth* and *gaggle* describe groups of things, particularly animals.

Below are other words used to name animal groups. Some of the words are not used much anymore, but they do make our language more colorful and vivid.

Write a sentence using each bold word as a group of animals. Then write a second sentence using a different meaning for the bold word.

Example: a **bale** of turtles — Joey found a *bale* of turtles near the lake. Marti fed the cows a *bale* of hay.

1. a **band** of gorillas ______________________________
2. a **brace** of ducks ______________________________
3. a **cast** of hawks ______________________________
4. a **charm** of goldfinches ______________________________
5. a **watch** of nightingales ______________________________
6. a **gang** of elks ______________________________
7. a **knot** of toads ______________________________
8. a **pride** of lions ______________________________
9. a **clutter** of cats ______________________________
10. a **leash** of foxes ______________________________
11. a **mob** of kangaroos ______________________________
12. a **pack** of wolves ______________________________
13. a **pod** of whales ______________________________
14. a **school** of fish ______________________________
15. a **leap** of leopards ______________________________

Name____________________________

As Cold As Ice Cream

A *simile* is a figure of speech that makes a comparison between two different nouns using *like* or *as.* Authors and poets use similes in their writing to make it more interesting.

Directions: Follow the steps below to create a simile about ice cream.

1. Write a flavor of ice cream on the first blank line in Part A and in Part B below. For example, *chocolate ice cream* and *butter pecan ice cream.*
2. On the next blank line in each part, compare each flavor with another noun. Then on the last blank line, explain why the flavor is like that noun. For example: *Chocolate ice cream* is like *a millionaire* because *it's rich. Butter pecan ice cream* is like *pudding* because *it is so creamy.*
3. Next piece the important words together to form a comparative sentence, then write it on the line provided. For example: *Chocolate ice cream is as rich as a millionaire. Butter pecan ice cream is as creamy as pudding.*
4. Choose one of your comparative sentences to use as the first line of a poem about your ice cream. Think of additional comparative sentences to add to your poem; then write your poem on the lines of the ice-cream cone pattern at the right.
5. Color the outer edges of the ice cream to make it resemble the flavor that you wrote about in your poem.

Part A:

____________ is like ____________ because ____________.

Comparative Sentence: ______________________________

Part B:

____________ is like ____________ because ____________.

Comparative Sentence: ______________________________

Name ______________________________

Feline Phrases

Have a little feline fun with the following activity on idioms! Each sentence below contains an *idiom*—a phrase whose words taken together often have little or nothing to do with the meaning of the words taken one by one. Each ball of yarn below is labeled with a definition of one of the common idioms listed in the center of the page. Use the context clues found in each sentence to match the idiom with a definition in one of the balls of yarn. Write the letter of the corresponding ball of yarn on the appropriate blank beside each sentence.

_____ 1. We wanted to surprise Lisa with a going-away party, but Stephen let the cat out of the bag.

_____ 2. When Kari saw Sara with a dress like hers, she called her a copycat.

_____ 3. "Curiosity killed the cat," Jerry's mother reminded, when she found Jerry searching the closets just before his birthday.

_____ 4. Kacie was a fraidy-cat because she cried every time her mother dropped her off at school.

_____ 5. "Holy cats! I just saw a ghost!" exclaimed Maggie.

_____ 6. When Tommy beat the fastest boy in the race, he looked like the cat that ate the canary.

_____ 7. Everybody on the playground got soaked when it suddenly started raining cats and dogs.

_____ 8. Cindy tried every solution to the puzzle that she could think of because she knew there was more than one way to skin a cat.

_____ 9. The principal was hoping to get some fat cats to help pay for the new playground equipment.

_____ 10. Mrs. Lindsay asked Thad if the cat had his tongue when he wouldn't respond to her question.

A — a shy person; someone who is easily frightened

B — wealthy people

C — someone who copies another person's work or manners

D — to seem very self-satisfied; to look as if you've had a great success

E — to tell about something that is supposed to be a secret

F — expressing strong feelings of pleasure, astonishment, or anger

G — several different ways of reaching the same goal

H — being so nosy will get you in trouble

I — to rain very hard; come down in torrents

J — not speaking; being silent

Name ______________________________

You Can Teach An Old Dog New Tricks!

The English language has thousands of *idioms,* or expressions that are peculiar to a people or their language. These short phrases are often confusing because the meaning of the phrase has little to do with the meaning of each individual word when taken separately.

Directions: In each bone below, write what you think each idiom means. Then illustrate its meaning in the space provided above each bone.

1. The new teacher raises her voice quite often, but *her bark is worse than her bite*.
2. When Ralph's car got stolen, he realized what a *dog-eat-dog* city it was.
3. Poor Anne-Marie. With that beat-up car and a house that's falling down, she leads a *dog's life*.
4. Sheila can't make it to the concert tonight. She is *as sick as a dog*.
5. I forgot to feed the cat and do my homework, so now I'm *in the doghouse*.
6. I asked Aunt Martha if I could teach her how to send an e-mail message on the computer, but she refused. *You can't teach an old dog new trick*s.

Sounds Simply Sensational!

Part One: Jazz up the following sentences with words that have the same beginning sounds. Then complete the activities in Part Two.

1. ________________ Patricia purchased ____________ ______________ for ______________________.

2. Joyce just ________________ a jet for __________________ so that she could ____________ her ___________________.

3. Did _______________ Dan _______________ the __________________ to _________________?

4. Matthew made __________________ on ____________________.

5. __________________ Clancy can't ___________________ 'cause his __________________ ______________________.

Part Two: Think of a letter other than *p, j, d, m,* or *c.* Write this letter in the blank below. Then use a dictionary to help you find nouns, verbs, and adjectives that begin with this new letter. Write the words that you find in the categories below.

____
letter

Nouns	**Verbs**	**Adjectives**
____________	____________	____________
____________	____________	____________
____________	____________	____________
____________	____________	____________
____________	____________	____________

Now, on the lines below, write several silly sentences using as many of these words as you can!

1. ____

2. ____

3. ____

4. ____

5. ____

Name ____________________

Autumn Alliteration

Alliteration is when beginning consonant sounds are repeated in words (see the example shown).

Below are twelve sentences filled with alliteration. The words in each one have been scrambled, and the capital letters and end punctuation marks have been removed. Rewrite each sentence so that it makes sense. Add capital letters and punctuation marks where needed. Use a dictionary to look up any words you do not know.

Example: took tackling teams tables two turns <u>*Two teams took turns tackling tables.*</u>

1. fumbled freddie football the foolishly frantic
____
2. scratched scarecrow's the scouts scalp
____
3. juggled jake the joyfully jack-o'-lanterns
____
4. repair randy's required rake rusty
____
5. hefty harvey's has helen harvest helped handle
____
6. september silly about scamper squirrels and scurry in
____
7. lost leaves lots lovely luster their of
____
8. clyde clad clothing classy in is colorful
____
9. wet went wednesday's weather westward
____
10. prize private polly's produced patch pumpkins
____
11. tommy tomatoes to topic told teachers on talk of the
____
12. both bob bought books barb's of bound
____

Name ____

A Barrel Of Words

One of the words in each of the barrels below does not belong. First write a category name for each group of words on the line below the barrel. Then circle the word that does not fit that category. The first one is done for you.

1.
apple
orange
strawberry
banana
pepper (circled)

fruits

2.
apple
button
playing card
tennis ball
nickel

____

3.
apple
tar
crown
ring
blond hair

____

4.
apple
alarm clock
phone
bell
doorbell

____

5.
apple
butter
fish
jelly
pie

____

6.
apple
paper
rubber
telephone
syrup

____

7.
apple
soda
candy
salt
ice cream

____

8.
apple
ice
carrot
pretzel
pudding

____

9.
apple
cherry-flavored gum
rose
stop sign
snow

____

10.
apple
notebook
potato
person
snake

____

11.
apple
person
needle
hurricane
camera

____

12.
apple
lobster
turtle
coconut
peanut

____

Name ____________________

Scientific Analogies

An **analogy** compares a likeness between two objects that are otherwise unlike. Read the analogies below. Observe each one carefully and try to find the missing word for each one. The clue is to discover how the words in the first pair go together.

Example: *Dog* is to *puppy* as *cat* is to ____________.

A puppy is a baby dog, so what is a baby cat? If you guessed *kitten* you are absolutely correct!

Now use your scientific brainpower to determine the clues that will help you solve each analogy below!

1. *Heart* is to *circulation* as *stomach* is to ____________.
2. *Rodent* is to *mammal* as *beetle* is to ____________.
3. *C* is to *Celsius* as *F* is to ____________.
4. *Incisor* is to *cut* as *molar* is to ____________.
5. *Elephant* is to *tusk* as *rattlesnake* is to ____________.
6. *Moon* is to *satellite* as *Earth* is to ____________.
7. *Lunar* is to *moon* as *solar* is to ____________.
8. *Oxygen* is to *inhale* as *carbon dioxide* is to ____________.
9. *Drizzle* is to *downpour* as *flurry* is to ____________.
10. *Buffalo* is to *mammal* as *alligator* is to ____________.
11. *Lobster* is to *shell* as *trout* is to ____________.
12. *Cabbage* is to *leaf* as *carrot* is to ____________.
13. *Galaxy* is to *star* as *forest* is to ____________.
14. *Butterfly* is to *nectar* as *mosquito* is to ____________.
15. *Spider* is to *invertebrate* as *whale* is to ____________.
16. *Bee* is to *swarm* as *wolf* is to ____________.
17. *Brain* is to *nervous system* as *artery* is to ____________.
18. *Wood* is to *solid* as *air* is to ____________.

Investigating Analogies

An **analogy** compares a likeness between two objects that are otherwise unlike. Read the analogies below. Act like a detective and try to find the missing word for each one. The clue is to discover how the words in the first pair go together.

> **Example:** *Goose* is to *gosling* as *cow* is to __________.
>
> A gosling is a baby goose, so what is a baby cow? If you guessed *calf* you are absolutely correct!

Now use your detective brainpower to determine the clues that will help you solve each analogy below!

1. *Duck* is to *waddle* as *frog* is to ______________________________.
2. *Hot dog* is to *eat* as *milk* is to ______________________________.
3. *Water* is to *wet* as *desert* is to ______________________________.
4. *Pickle* is to *sour* as *candy* is to ______________________________.
5. *Boat* is to *water* as *airplane* is to ______________________________.
6. *Skin* is to *humans* as *scales* are to ______________________________.
7. *Flour* is to *wheat* as *sawdust* is to ______________________________.
8. *Dog* is to *bark* as *cat* is to ______________________________.
9. *Perfume* is to *nose* as *music* is to ______________________________.
10. *Potato* is to *vegetable* as *apple* is to ______________________________.
11. *Grass* is to *green* as *sky* is to ______________________________.
12. *Spaghetti* is to *Italian* as *taco* is to ______________________________.
13. *Baseball* is to *throw* as *soccer ball* is to ______________________________.
14. *Curtains* are to *windows* as *sunglasses* are to ______________________________.
15. *Apple* is to *skin* as *nut* is to ______________________________.
16. *Foot* is to *big toe* as *hand* is to ______________________________.
17. *Shower* is to *bathroom* as *refrigerator* is to ______________________________.
18. *Lawyer* is to *courtroom* as *teacher* is to ______________________________.
19. *Noise* is to *loud* as *whisper* is to ______________________________.
20. *Smell* is to *nose* as *touch* is to ______________________________.

Name ____

How Sweet It Is!

Sweeten your vocabulary by using a dictionary or other resource book to find the definition for each dessert word below. Record the definition in the space provided on each recipe card.

1. Custard

2. Trifle

3. Meringue

4. Soufflé

5. Torte

6. Tart

7. Strudel

8. Baklava

9. Savarin

10. Cruller

11. Sorbet

12. Compote

Name ____________________

Things for You 2 Do 2-Day

Mama Listoni has made a list of what she needs to do today and of several things she needs from the store. Read through this list and then answer the following questions below to help Mama Listoni out!

- Go to the dentist.
- To avoid traffic, take the back way.
- Pay with a credit card.
- Ask for teacher's comments on Amy's progress.
- See if she suggests any good books to help make Amy's reading comprehension a success.
- Contact Amy's teacher.
- Pick up a few products from the market: cactus, lettuce, insect repellent.

1. List all of the two-syllable words whose first syllable has a short *e* sound:
   ________, ________, ________
2. List all of the two-syllable words whose second syllable has a short *e* sound:
   ________, ________, ________,
   ________, ________, ________
3. List all of the two-syllable words whose first syllable has a short *a* sound:
   ________, ________
4. List all of the two-syllable words whose first syllable has a short *o* sound:
   ________, ________, ________,
   ____

Now make your own list of two-syllable short-vowel words!

____

____

____

____

____

____

____

____

Fourth-Grade Parent Page

Grammar, Usage, & Mechanics

This school year is a very important transition year for your child. Basic grammar is emphasized to an extent not previously experienced in grades K–3. Good grammar skills are essential to tackle the increased amount of writing done by fourth graders. Today, many school districts across the country are giving their fourth graders standardized writing tests, for which proper grammar use is a graded part of the overall test score.

While writing paragraphs, fourth graders have many opportunities to practice good garmmar. Eventually, fourth graders are assigned longer compositions and written reports on a variety of topics. Fourth graders will be asked to write personal narratives, comparisons and contrasts, letters, stories, and descriptive passages. Creative writing in many forms is also encouraged. Through these longer assignments, grammar skills—such as punctuation, parts of speech, and paragraph structure—are reinforced.

Your fourth grader will encounter the following skills:

- Parts of speech: common and proper nouns, pronouns, verbs, adverbs, adjectives, prepositions, and conjunctions (For example, and, but, or)
- Subject/verb agreement
- Possessives (For example, Aunt Mary's hat, the students' papers)
- Abbreviations
- Capitalization: titles, magazines, books, proper nouns
- Punctuation: commas in a series, quotation marks, apostrophes
- Simple and compound sentences
- Sentence structure: compound subjects and predicates

To ensure a smooth transitional fourth-grade year, try the grammar activities on the next page for developing good home-study skills.

Let's Journal!

To foster a love of writing, why not invest in a simple journal or diary for your child's daily use? This can be as simple as a spiral notebook or a fancier version with a lock and key. Invest in two such journals, and let your child be inspired by your own journaling! As your child journals, have her apply one of the skills highlighted on the following pages to one of her daily entries. Applying a new skill to a fun-filled journal entry can reinforce use of commas, quotation marks, etc., in a much more memorable and personal way.

Oops!

Reading the local paper can be fun, especially when you are looking for mistakes! Many newspapers are rushed to meet daily deadlines, and editors *do* make mistakes. Employ your child as the newspaper's newest "editor," and focus on finding errors. Have your child look for errors in mechanics that got by the copy editor of the paper. Have her check out a specific section of the newspaper each week. Find any mistakes on the sports page or the front page? She might be surprised by how many mistakes *the adults* make!

Sign Language

Carpooling? Don't let your child's grammar skills go idle at each red light. Instead, create a "Blunder Book" out of a simple spiral notebook. Attach a pen with string or cord. As you pass gas stations, fast-food restaurants, or other establishments with do-it-yourself signs out front, have your child record all the errors she finds on signs.

Name ____

Name That Noun!

Directions: Underline all of the common nouns in each sentence below. Next draw a picture for each sentence in the box provided for it. Then rewrite each sentence by replacing all of the common nouns in it with proper nouns that match its picture.

Example: The **girl** went to the **city. Princess Meg** went to **Paris.**

1.

1. The pet ate the food.

____.

2.

2. I got a toy on the holiday.

____.

3.

3. The boy used soap to wash the car.

____.

4.

4. The city is in a state.

____.

5.

5. The president went to the store.

____.

Name ____

Motion Picture Pronouns

Sue and Sean love to go to the movies, but without using the proper pronouns, how will they know where to sit?

Directions: Know these pronouns: I, me, we, us, he, him, she, her, it, they, them, and you. Read each pair of sentences. Next, circle the pronoun in the second sentence. Finally, underline the word or words it refers to in the first sentence.

Hint: A pronoun is a word used in place of a noun or nouns.

1. Sue caught the keys. Sue gave them to Sean.
2. Sue and Sean drove to the store. They bought a newspaper.
3. Sue wanted to look up the movie times. They didn't start for an hour.
4. Sean was hungry. He ate before the movie.
5. Sue and Sean picked up a few friends on the way. They all had a great time.

Now read the following paragraphs. Underline each pronoun. Above each pronoun, write the noun. The first one is done for you.

John loves to go to the beach. (John) He could go every day. He loves to surf and walk on the beach. One day, while surfing, a shark swam under his surfboard. It scared him enough to keep him away from the ocean.

John realized that sharks won't bother him, unless they are hungry. "Boy," thought John when he got back on the beach, "that scare would really make a great movie!"

Name ____________________

Food Fit For A King!

King Ferdinand is quite fond of food. Each day throughout the week, he writes his court cook a note. Find the nouns and adjectives in each note below (do not include articles). Then write them in the correct serving dishes below. Use a dictionary for help, if needed.

1 *Monday*
The pheasant was perfectly cooked! The queen was fond of the tender turnips and warm, white bread.

2 *Tuesday*
Meat pie would provide an appetizing dinner. But I am so hungry now! Send me a platter of sugary quinces and cooked apples.

3 *Wednesday*
The tarts were the tastiest! Were they made with nuts and dates? I would like mincemeat pie for lunch tomorrow.

4 *Thursday*
Prepare the Great Hall for a royal feast! Be certain to serve the freshest fish, the most savory sausage, and the finest fowl.

5 *Friday*
The cider you served was as refreshing as the trickling brook beside the manor. I toast the apple orchard!

6 *Saturday*
Lady Margaret of Devonshire will visit on Sunday. Treat her to a table with the most sumptuous delights.

7 *Sunday*
Please bring the custards to the fireside. Young Edward has engaged me in a grueling game of chess.

Name ________________________________ Parts of speech: adjectives

Feast On These Descriptions!

Cotton candy, ice cream, and hot dogs—how would you describe foods like these to a king of long ago?

Directions: Think about each food shown below. On each numbered picture, write an adjective describing how each food (1) looks, (2) tastes, (3) smells, (4) feels, and (5) sounds as it is eaten.

Example: An ice-cream cone is (1) creamy and crunchy, (2) sweet, (3) flavorful, (4) cold, and (5) quiet.

Name ______________________________

Victory With Verbs

Monica Seles is a bona fide tennis legend. But a tennis ball isn't all she knows how to handle. See how verbs help her describe how she plays her action-filled sport!

Directions: Read the following sentences. Underline the verb(s) and write an *A* if it describes an action or a *B* if it describes a state of being.

A verb is a word that expresses an *action* or a state of *being*.
Action: jump, hit, kick
Being: is, are, was, were, seems

1. At 17, Monica Seles became the youngest women's tennis player to be ranked #1 in the world. __________
2. She won championship after championship. __________
3. She was an awesome talent. __________
4. Then Monica had a few setbacks. __________
5. After two years she staged a triumphant return! __________
6. Now she's playing again and winning. __________
7. Aside from playing, Monica stays busy working with handicapped athletes. __________
8. Monica is a role model for many people. __________

Try This: Write a five- or six-sentence paragraph about *your* favorite sport on a separate sheet of paper. To make it more exciting, use as many action verbs as possible!

Ready Reference

Common Verb Tenses

Past Tense
Indicates an action that happened at a specific time in the past.

Mike *liked* to go to the beach.

He *went* almost every day.

Present Tense
Indicates an action that is happening now, or that happens regularly.

Liz *likes* walking in the park.

Stephanie *walks* with her each afternoon.

Future Tense
Indicates an action that is going to take place. Future tense is formed by adding *shall* or *will* before the main verb.

Debra *will go* to lunch with us tomorrow.

Don and Cory *will meet* us at the restaurant.

Special Verb Tenses

Past Perfect Tense
Indicates an action that began and was completed in the past. Past perfect tense is formed by adding *had* before the main verb.

Becky *had worked* for over three hours without a break.

Present Perfect Tense
Indicates an action that is still going on. Present perfect tense is formed by using *has* or *have* before the main verb.

Thad *has slept* for eight hours.

Future Perfect Tense
Indicates an action that will start in the future and end at a specific time in the future. Future perfect tense is formed by adding *will have* or *shall have* before the main verb.

Peggy *will have walked* on the treadmill for 30 minutes.

Name ____________________

Star-Studded Action Heroes

Directions: Design your own action hero inside the star-framed box below. Make your character as large and colorful as possible. Then look at the list of words at the bottom of this sheet. Circle the 15 words that are action verbs. Then choose five of the circled words. Use each chosen word in a different sentence.

gallop	be	see	leap	understand
is	think	explode	was	save
run	carried	jump	wall	grew
will	flew	am	sleep	were
eat	are	wonder	life	sun

Name ______________________________

Pleasing Pancakes

Chef Geoff knows the king absolutely flips over pancakes! So just how does Geoff make these king-pleasing pancakes? Complete the activity below to find out.

Directions: Circle the adverb in each sentence below. Draw an arrow to the word that the adverb is describing. Then color the pancake to show if the adverb is telling *where, how,* or *when.* The first one is done for you.

	Where	How	When
1. The stove temperature should be fairly hot.	A	F	L
2. This first pancake is completely burned!	B	C	M
3. Oh, no! The batter has spilled everywhere.	A	W	Q
4. The king is terribly fond of fresh berries on his pancakes.	P	R	V
5. Pancakes must be flipped properly.	X	Y	I
6. This pancake is almost done.	E	L	H
7. The king often eats three or more stacks of pancakes.	S	K	E
8. Chocolate chip pancakes are quite tasty.	J	U	G
9. The king is positively picky about his pancakes!	A	V	Z
10. I always cook my pancakes to perfection!	T	O	Y
11. Here is a new stack.	E	C	A
12. A batch of fresh pancakes will be made tomorrow.	M	K	R

Write the letter that you colored for each number shown below.

___ ___ ___ ___   ___ ___ ___ ___ ___ ___ ___ ___ ___ !
9 11 4 5   2 3 12 7 1 8 6 6 10

Ready Reference

Capitalization Rules

To *capitalize* means to begin a word with a capital letter. The following items should always be capitalized:

- **the first word in a sentence**
  We went to the store yesterday.

- **proper nouns**
  - **names of people**
    Beverly Cleary
  - **geographic names**
    New Jersey
    Jupiter
    Europe
    Hillside Street
    Mississippi River
  - **historic events**
    Stamp Act
    Civil War
  - **names of days or months**
    Wednesday
    December
  - **national and local holidays**
    Easter

- **proper adjectives**
  Spanish
  American

- **the pronoun I**
  When I heard the news, I shouted for joy.

- **titles and initials**
  Captain Kirk
  Mrs. Krolikowski
  R. J. Hayes

- **words used as names**
  Will you ask Dad if we can go to the movies?
  We saw Aunt Ellie at the park.

- **first word in the greeting and closing of a letter**
  Dear Julie,
  My dear friend,

- **titles of written works (first word, last word, all main words)**
  Sports Illustrated for Kids
  The Wizard of Oz

- **abbreviations**
  P.T.A.
  USA
  Dr.

Name that Address!

Help your local mail carrier by learning to address the following envelopes properly.

Directions: Correct the items that are wrong on the envelopes below. Write your corrections on each envelope.

Rules

1. Begin each important word in the name of a town, city, state, or country with a capital letter.
2. Begin each important word in the names of streets and their abbreviations with capital letters.

Susan Johnson
310 grave ave
Cape Canaveral, FL 32391

____

Jane Doe
4510 Lester Ct.
merritt island, fl 42891

____

Now that you're such an address expert, write a real letter to a friend or family member and address your own envelope. Don't forget the stamp! Practice here first:

Dr. Drey
45 Diamond Rd.
Las Vegas, nv 85021

____

Jerry Parker
36 Young Ave.
orlando, fl 36298

____

Name ______________________________

Congratulations On Your Graduation!

Society Sarah is finally graduating from charm school. Her invitations have to be just "write." Help Sarah write the perfect invitations by reading the rules below.

Rules

1. Begin each part of the name of a person with a capital letter.
2. Begin the title of a person with a capital letter.
3. Use a period after an abbreviation of an initial or title.

Directions: Help Sarah correct the following names and titles so that she can send out invitations to her graduation. Use abbreviations for titles.

1. mister rogers ____________
2. senator richard ____________
3. doctor zhivago ____________
4. miss sara j burns ____________
5. ms helen rita ____________
6. governor doppler ____________

Now that you've helped her capitalize proper names, write these sentences correctly for Sarah. This information will be inside her invitations.

7. senator johnson will be speaking at my party.

   ____

8. ms mariah carey will be singing my favorite song.

   ____

9. doctor doolittle will be performing with animals.

   ____

10. marvin the magician will be doing magic tricks.

    ____

11. mr magoo will be drawing caricatures of all the guests.

    ____

12. governor sparkler will be setting off fireworks at the end of the night.

    ____

Name ______________________________

Addresses Please!

Even make-believe characters need addresses! Make up an address for each character on the lines of each envelope below. Make sure that each line of the address includes at least one abbreviation and relates to the character named on the envelope (see the example).

Bob B. Socks
117 Foot St.
Shoe, NY 00117

1\. Mr. Big B. Wolf

____

____

2\. Mr. Frank N. Stein

____

____

3\. Mr. Tom Turkey

____

____

4\. Mr. San T. Claws

____

____

5\. Ms. Tooth Fairy

____

____

6\. Mr. E. Ster Bunny

____

____

Try This: Draw and color a special stamp on each envelope above. Design each stamp so that it represents that particular character.

Name____

Capital Ideas

Fill in the information requested below. Use encyclopedias and other reference materials if you need extra help. All of the answers will begin with a capital letter.

1. Write your full name. ____________________
2. Name one of the 50 states in the United States of America. ____________________
3. What is the title of your favorite book? ____________________
4. Write the names of your two favorite months of the year. ____________________
5. Name the five Great Lakes. ____________________
6. What is the abbreviation for the Central Intelligence Agency? ____________________
7. Name two streets that are in your neighborhood. ____________________
8. What war began in the United States in 1775? ____________________
9. What holiday is celebrated on December 25? ____________________
10. Name the seven days of the week. ____________________

    ____
11. Who is the current president of the United States of America? ____________________
12. What day comes after Tuesday? ____________________
13. What is your favorite holiday? ____________________
14. What state is north of Oregon? ____________________
15. What is the title of your favorite magazine? ____________________
16. Name the capital of Virginia. ____________________
17. What month comes after June on the calendar? ____________________
18. Name a famous war in United States history. ____________________
19. What is the name of your school? ____________________
20. Who wrote the book *Charlotte's Web*? ____________________
21. Name a mountain range. ____________________
22. What war began in the United States in 1861? ____________________
23. Name the planet that is closest to the sun. ____________________
24. What are two of the world's oceans? ____________________

Try This: Write a short story using as many of the words above as you can.

Ready Reference

Punctuation Rules

Use a period:

- **at the end of a declarative sentence—a sentence that makes a statement**
  I enjoy playing basketball.
- **at the end of an imperative sentence—a sentence that makes a request**
  Please bring me that measuring cup.
- **after a person's initials**
  A. J. Wydell
- **after an abbreviation**
  Mrs. Jones
  Dr. McIntosh

Use a question mark:

- **at the end of an interrogative sentence—a sentence that asks a question**
  What number does Mike Smith wear?

Use an exclamation point:

- **to express strong feeling or emotion**
  Ouch!
  Leave me alone!
  Wow!

Use quotation marks:

- **to show a direct quotation**
  Jennifer said, "I am going to the movies with Carrie."
- **to show the titles of written works—poems, stories, or songs**
  "America the Beautiful"

Use an apostrophe:

- **to show that one or more letters have been left out to form a contraction**
  can't—can not
  won't—will not
  don't—do not
- **to show possession**
  Carolyn's keys are in the car.
  The boys' game was over an hour ago.

Use a hyphen:

- **to divide a word between syllables at the end of a line**
  The automobile sales-
  man is named Mr. Sears.
- **to join parts of some compound words**
  drive-in, father-in-law
- **to write number words from 21 through 99**
  twenty-one

Ready Reference

Punctuation Rules

Use a comma:

- **to separate items in a date or address**
  August 22, 1970
  Bardstown, Kentucky 40051
- **after the greeting and closing of a letter**
  Dear Andrew,
  Yours truly,
- **to separate words or phrases in a series**
  Sharon bought eggs, bread, and milk at the store.
- **with quotations to set off the exact words of the speaker from the rest of the sentence**
  Jimmy said, "I want to visit my niece in North Carolina."
- **to separate a noun of direct address from the rest of the sentence**
  Rob, did your team win the hockey game last night?
- **to separate a long clause or phrase from the independent clause following it**
  As I was walking on the beach, I found several conch shells.
  When Jeff bought his new car, he sold his old one.
- **to join two simple sentences into a compound sentence**
  Madeline went to sleep, but Mackenzie stayed up to watch television.
- **to set off an appositive**
  (a word or phrase that renames the noun or pronoun before it)
  Adrienne, a great gymnast, won first place at the meet.
- **with an interrupter** (a word, phrase, or clause that interrupts the main thought of a sentence) Swimming, I feel, is the best exercise.
  In the end, however, Carlin couldn't come to the party.
- **when writing the last name first**
  Lundein, Gregory

Use a colon:

- **after the salutation of a business letter**
  Dear Mr. Metcalf:
- **in writing times**
  3:45
- **before a list or series**
  There were three contestants: Angela, Sarah, and Jackie.
- **after the speaker in a play or dialogue**
  Nicholas: When are we leaving?
  Alex: We leave in about 20 minutes.

Use a semicolon:

- **between the independent clauses of a compound sentence when a conjunction is not used**
  Martin washed the car; John waxed it.
  Beverly and Michael went to Hawaii; they stayed there for two weeks.

Name ____

The Rematch

The Brushin' Up Paint Company guys are taking a break from their work by reading a favorite book. It's called *The Hare And The Tortoise: A Rematch*. According to this book, who wins the second run of this classic race? To find out, follow the directions in the box.

Make each **correct** sentence into a tortoise.
Make each **incorrect** sentence into a hare.
Then rewrite the sentence correctly on the back of this page.

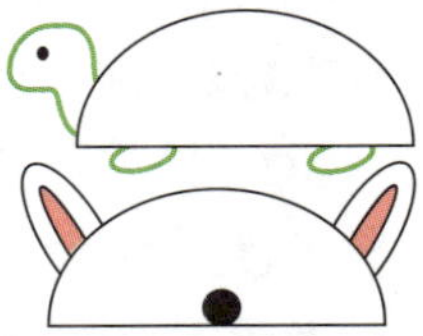

1. My dad loves to cook and, my mom loves to fix cars.
2. Cindy loves chocolate, but Katie prefers vanilla.
3. Even though I forgot to remind her Lea still studied for the test.
4. To help me be less nervous, Mom practiced my speech with me.
5. I packed a pen a pencil case and two books in my backpack.
6. Shelby asked Mark, Brendan, and Maya to be on her team.
7. Yes we will be home on Friday, night.
8. Oh did the game start already?
9. Diane, I'm sorry I didn't laugh at your joke.
10. What day will you be here, Caleb?
11. I've been expecting you Larry since 5:00.
12. Billy the funniest kid, in our class has read 11 riddle books.
13. Mr. Yountz, the best coach in the league, spoke to our class.
14. A huge hungry furry animal is at the back fence!

To find out who won the race, count the number of tortoises and hares above. The one with the greater number is the winner.

Name____

Carnival Commas

Everyone has fun at the carnival, but it takes a real punctuation pro to describe the experience accurately! See if you can help the following sentences be more descriptive by using commas correctly. After the comma carnival, it's off to a birthday party!

Rules:

1. Use a comma before the words *but* and *or* when two sentences are combined.
2. Use a comma after the words *yes* and *no* when they begin a statement.
3. Use a comma to separate three or more words in a series.
4. Use a comma between a quotation and the rest of the sentence.

Directions: Place commas where needed.

1. Jerry was reluctant but he rode the roller coaster with his friends.
2. Susan bought popcorn candy apples and hot dogs there.
3. John asked the conductor "Can you speed up the train?"
4. "No" said the conductor politely.
5. Everyone had fun at the carnival but all good things must come to an end.

Now, read the following diary entry and place commas where they belong.

Dear Diary,

Yes I had the greatest day today. It was my eleventh birthday and I ate cake ice cream and pizza! All my best friends were there but Sarah didn't show up. That left Ashley Kate Loretta Keisha Sally and Pam. What a crowd! Everyone had a great time but I think we all ate too much. People said "Oh my stomach hurts" as often as they said "Happy Birthday." Next year I think I'll skip the pizza—no maybe the ice cream!

Name ____________________

Show & Tell Possessives

The students in Miss Richard's class are discussing where animals live. Rewrite each phrase, using a possessive noun. The first one is done for you.

	Noun	Possessive Noun
Singular	girl	girl's
Plural ending in -s	boys	boys'
Plural not ending in -s	men	men's

1. the house for a dog dog's house
2. the tree of the iguana ____________________
3. the web of the spiders ____________________
4. the stream of the turtles ____________________
5. the branch of the bird ____________________
6. the darkened crevice of the eel ____________________
7. the pride of the children ____________________
8. the den of the fox ____________________

Name ____

Antsy Apostrophes

It's springtime, and Alvin Ant is getting *antsy!* He needs help finding a path to the picnic basket filled with food. Read the sentences below. Then, beginning at **START,** color a path showing the correct use of the word *ant.* Use the Color Code below to show the words that are singular possessive and plural possessive. Use a different color to show the ones that are not possessive. The first one is done for you.

Color Code

singular possessive = pink

plural possessive = purple

1. Ants' homes are often underground.
2. Worker ________ are all female.
3. An ________ doesn't need to work out; it can lift things 50 times heavier than its body!
4. An ________ body has three main parts.
5. ________ nests can be made from tree leaves.
6. ________ deserve straight A's for their work effort!
7. Some ________ jobs include building nests, searching for food, and caring for the young.
8. The size of an ________ colony varies from a dozen to a million members.
9. ________ outer skeletons are hard, shell-like coverings.
10. A baby ________ room is called a nursery.
11. In some species, a soldier ________ chief job is to defend the colony from enemies.
12. ________ aren't all the same size.

START

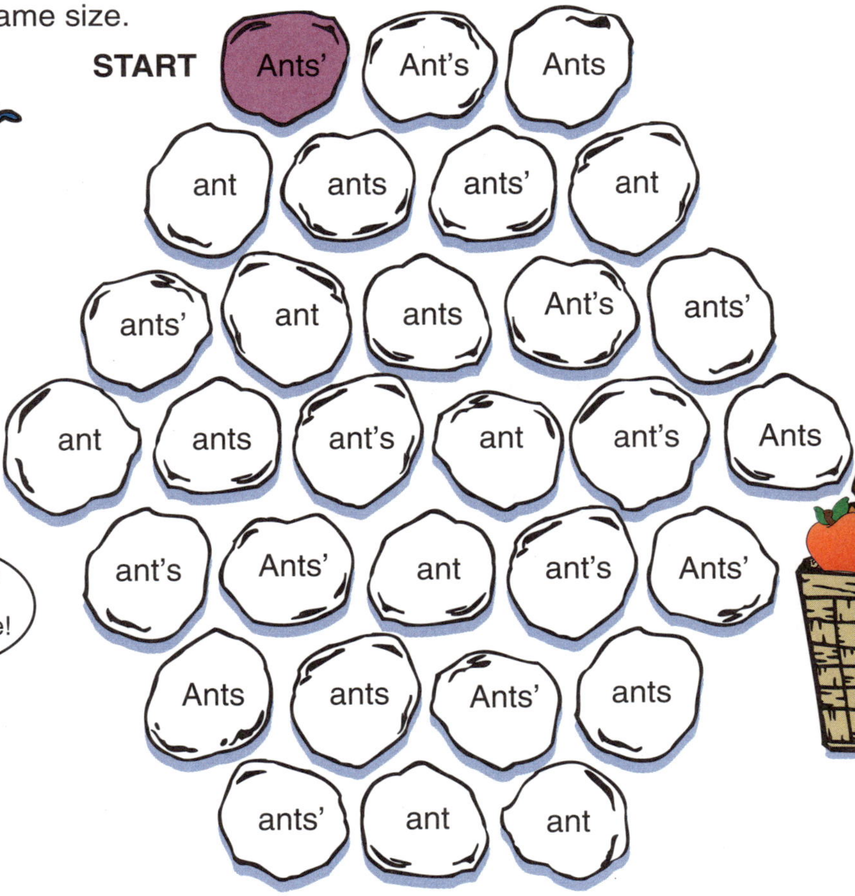

Name ______________________________

Adam's Apostrophe Mix-Up

Adam has written a report on sharks. However, he gets confused when using apostrophes. Sometimes he forgets to use them, puts them in the wrong place, or uses them when he shouldn't. Circle his mistakes and put the corrections in the spaces below.

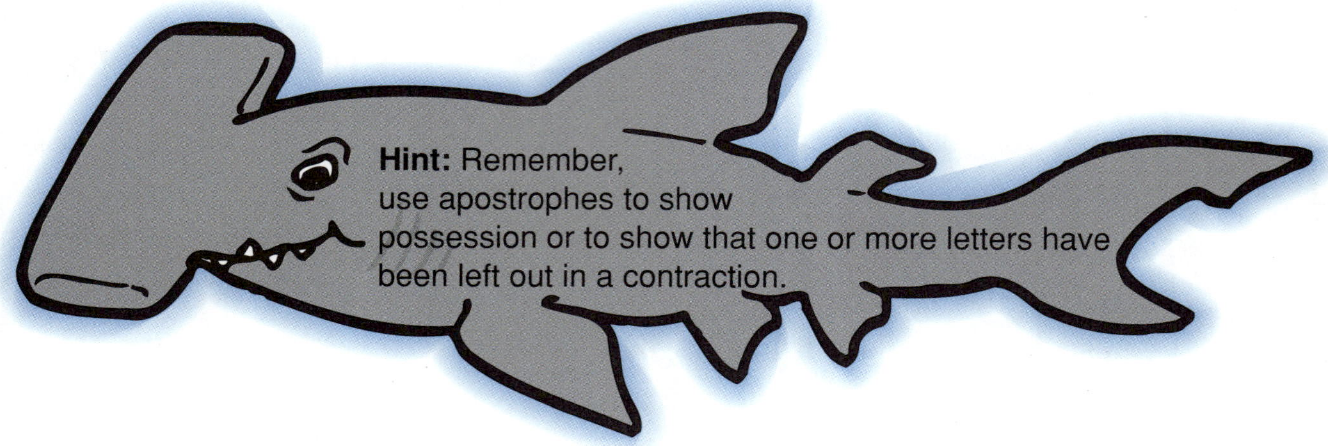

Hint: Remember,
use apostrophes to show
possession or to show that one or more letters have
been left out in a contraction.

There are many types of sharks. A very rare type is the megamouth shark. Only twelve have been spotted worldwide. Id love to see one because even though its large, it is rather timid.

Another shark I found interesting was the hammerhead shark. Theres no shortage of these sharks. Theyre usually not found close to shore; they prefer the deeper water. Sighting's of these sharks occur mostly in tropical water. They usually are not aggressive. They are not considered dangerous by divers, but a few humans' may have been attacked by this shark.

The thresher shark is a strange-looking creature. The length of it's tail is about the same as its bodys length. It likes to stay in the deep water. Its been known to use its tail to injure or kill its prey, usually schools of fish. It has not been known to attack humans.

The whale shark is the last shark Ill talk about. It's a gentle giant. It can grow to sixty feet in length. It is most commonly seen in the Indian Ocean. The whale sharks diet typically consists of small bait fish and plankton, but it will eat bigger fish at times, like tuna.

Reading about the sharks characteristics was very interesting.

Name ______________________________

Animal Talk

Dana Dolots is assistant to the famous Dr. Dolittle. While Dana was caring for the doctor's pets during his spring vacation, she left a note for the doctor stating what each animal said. But Dana got so busy that she forgot to put quotation marks around the animals' exact words!

Directions: Read each statement below. Use a colored pencil to put quotation marks around the exact words of the speaker. Add other punctuation marks and capitalization if needed. Use the rules below to help you. The first one is done for you.

1. "The silk in my web is so strong that even the heavy dew of a spring morning cannot damage it," said the spider.
2. I said the puma can jump 12 to 15 feet straight up into a tree!
3. The polar bear bellowed My thick coat keeps me warm while I enjoy a good springtime sparring.
4. I use my stomach as a table remarked the sea otter. I place a rock on it so I can break open clam shells to get to the meat inside.
5. During the spring and summer I have about 300 spots that cover my coat so wolves, bears, and other prey can't see me as easily replied the fawn.
6. Don't you know that I faithfully follow my mother wherever she goes questioned the duckling.
7. I eventually leave the pond and turn into a frog cried the tadpole.
8. Cooling off on a warm spring or summer day is easy commented the bird. I dip my feet and legs into cool water.
9. The bee answered I help pollinate many beautiful flowers.
10. I've been called the world's finest engineer barked the beaver I build dams more than 8 feet high and 40 feet wide.

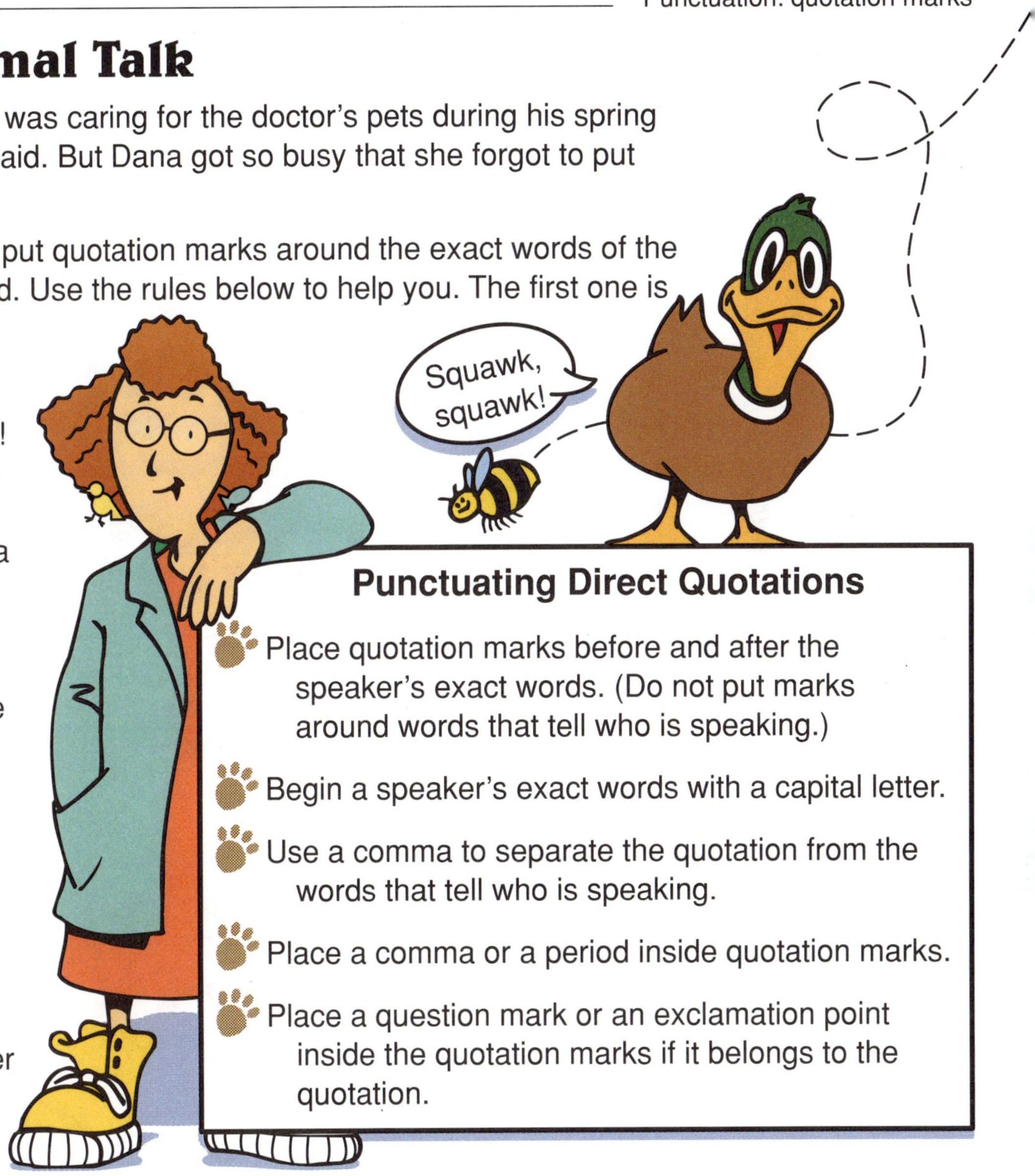

Punctuating Direct Quotations

- Place quotation marks before and after the speaker's exact words. (Do not put marks around words that tell who is speaking.)
- Begin a speaker's exact words with a capital letter.
- Use a comma to separate the quotation from the words that tell who is speaking.
- Place a comma or a period inside quotation marks.
- Place a question mark or an exclamation point inside the quotation marks if it belongs to the quotation.

Name ______________________________ Punctuation: Dialogue

You Ought To Be In The Comics!

Below are four cartoons that include some pretty famous people from the past. First draw yourself in each cartoon and answer the question(s) in the speech bubble. On another sheet of paper, rewrite each cartoon as a conversation between you and the famous person. Don't forget to use quotation marks and other punctuation marks correctly.

If you're a sports fan, then you know that I—James Naismith—played an important role in the invention of basketball. Would you rather play in or watch a sports event? Why?
As ruler of ancient Egypt, I, King Tutankhamen, never got to travel much. If you could go anywhere, where would you go and why would you choose this spot?
I'm Queen Victoria. I ruled Great Britain and Ireland from 1837 to 1901. Both the typewriter and the elevator were invented during my reign. Which was the more important invention? Why?
Hi, dearie! It's me, Mother Goose. Even though not everyone agrees that I ever existed, I'd still like to ask you a question. Would you rather write books for children or illustrate them? Why?

Name ____

What's On My Plate?

Read the sentence part on each plate. If the sentence part is a subject, color the plate blue. If it is a predicate, color the plate red.

1. ate all of the cookies — J
2. Tommy — P
3. my friend's father — E
4. Lisa and Joe — A
5. is teaching a new song to her students — H
6. the man wearing a hat — O
7. two big dogs — C
8. marched in the parade — T
9. the dog with the pink collar — K
10. dropped a penny on the ground — W
11. the girl with the long hair — C
12. arrived too late — B
13. my neighbor's car — S
14. are riding in the bus — D
15. had a milkshake — F
16. is swimming in the lake — G

What do police officers eat on their birthdays?

Color in the letter of each subject plate on this platter. Then read the riddle written above the platter. If you labeled all of the subjects correctly, the riddle's answer will be spelled out on the platter.

Dinner At The Diner

Mel has a new special on tonight's menu. Now he must change the sign in front of the diner to let everyone know. Help Mel by reading each sentence. If a sentence contains a compound subject, write its letter on the box at the left. If it contains a compound predicate, write its letter on the box at the right. Then follow the steps below to find out tonight's special.

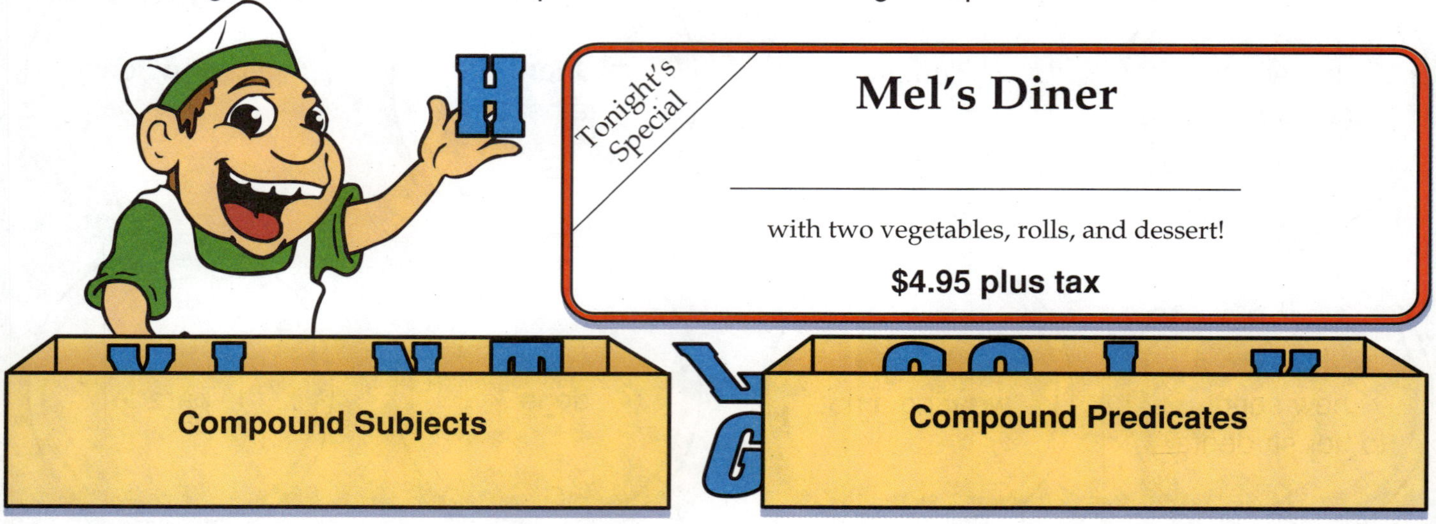

Tonight's Special
Mel's Diner
with two vegetables, rolls, and dessert!
$4.95 plus tax
Compound Subjects
Compound Predicates

(L) The cat and the dog fought over the food scraps.
(N) Tiny ants marched across the floor, climbed the cabinets, and crawled on the counter.
(S) Lions, tigers, and bears are at the zoo.
(C) Four cars turned off the street and followed the truck into the gas station.
(K) A beautiful rainbow stretched across the sky and soon disappeared.
(I) Mr. Edwards and Mr. Bowman are brothers.
(P) Mrs. Bray's nieces and nephews are visiting her.
(C) Bill looked at the clock and realized he would be late for his appointment.
(R) The new table and chairs looked so pretty in the dining room.
(E) Amy finished her math homework, studied for her science test, and practiced her spelling words.
(I) The neighbor's cat ran up the tree and wouldn't come down.
(W) Hot dogs and hamburgers are easy to grill.
(U) Brad, Angie, and Todd like to play volleyball on Saturdays.
(H) Sarah shopped at the mall and visited the ice-cream shop with her aunt.

When you're finished: If you correctly identified the compound subjects and predicates, one box above is now labeled with letters that spell tonight's special. On a piece of scrap paper, try to unscramble the letters on each box. When you think you know tonight's special, write it on Mel's sign.

Name ____

A Tasty Sentence Stew

Directions:

1. Read each sentence below. Write an "S" in the blank if the sentence is a **simple** sentence. Write a "C" if it's a **compound** sentence. Write an "R" if it's a **run-on** sentence.
2. Write the numbers for the simple sentences in the pot labeled "Simple." Do the same for the pots labeled "Compound" and "Run-On."
3. Find the sum of the numbers on each pot. Write each sum in the blank provided.
4. If the sentences are sorted correctly, the sum on each pot will be the same.

- A **simple** sentence is made up of one complete subject and one complete predicate.
- A **compound** sentence is two or more simple sentences joined by a comma and a conjunction.
- A **run-on** sentence is two or more sentences that run together without the proper punctuation to join them.

1. ____ Peter ate breakfast.
2. ____ I ate too much food I feel so sick.
3. ____ The chef prepared our meal.
4. ____ Corie likes spaghetti, but I would rather eat pizza.
5. ____ I like to cook I don't like to clean up the kitchen.
6. ____ My friend from school is eating dinner with us tonight.
7. ____ Warm milk makes me sleepy.
8. ____ You like french fries, but I prefer mashed potatoes.
9. ____ Carrots and peas are my favorite vegetables.
10. ____ Grandma baked a cake I had a piece of it.
11. ____ Grapes grow on a vine.
12. ____ Some apples are red, but bananas are yellow.
13. ____ Turn on the oven first, and then let it heat up.
14. ____ We can make lunch, or we can go out to eat.
15. ____ I dropped my ice-cream cone the clerk gave me a new one.
16. ____ My little brother ate breakfast and went outside to play.
17. ____ My fork and spoon dropped on the floor.
18. ____ I ordered a hamburger the waitress brought it to me.
19. ____ I ate all of my dinner, and Mom let me order dessert.
20. ____ I made a pizza it had cheese and pepperoni on it.

Name ____________________

Sentences Seasoned With Summertime!

You have to agree—summertime is a season filled with fun! Each sentence below is not only seasoned with a summertime activity but with a subject and verb, too.

Directions: Read each sentence below. Circle the subject in each one. Next decide if you *agree* or *disagree* with the verb used in each sentence. Color the sun that shows your decision. The first one is done for you.

	Agree	Disagree
1. Sally and Sam surf from sunrise to sunset.	B	Q
2. Hamburgers tastes terrific when served hot off a grill.	C	E
3. We roller-skate regularly near Rolling Rock River.	P	F
4. Wanda water-skis wonderfully.	R	L
5. The Higginses hikes high in the mountains each summer.	K	S
6. Gertrude grow wildflowers in her garden.	D	N
7. I rides horses at The Triple R Ranch.	Y	A
8. Bailey watches birds in his backyard.	Z	G
9. Carmen camps at her cousin's country cabin.	M	H
10. Terrel travel on a tour bus throughout Texas.	V	J
11. Sabrina says sunbathing is simply sensational.	U	X
12. Five friends fish at Fairview Farm.	I	B
13. They pack a picnic of pasta and pickles.	O	W

Write the letter that you colored for each number shown below.

___ ___ ___ ___ ___ ___   ___ ___   ___   ___ ___ ___ ___ ___   ___ ___ ___ ___ ___ ___!

5 11 9 9 2 4   12 5   7   5 11 3 2 4   5 2 7 5 13 6

Name ______________________________

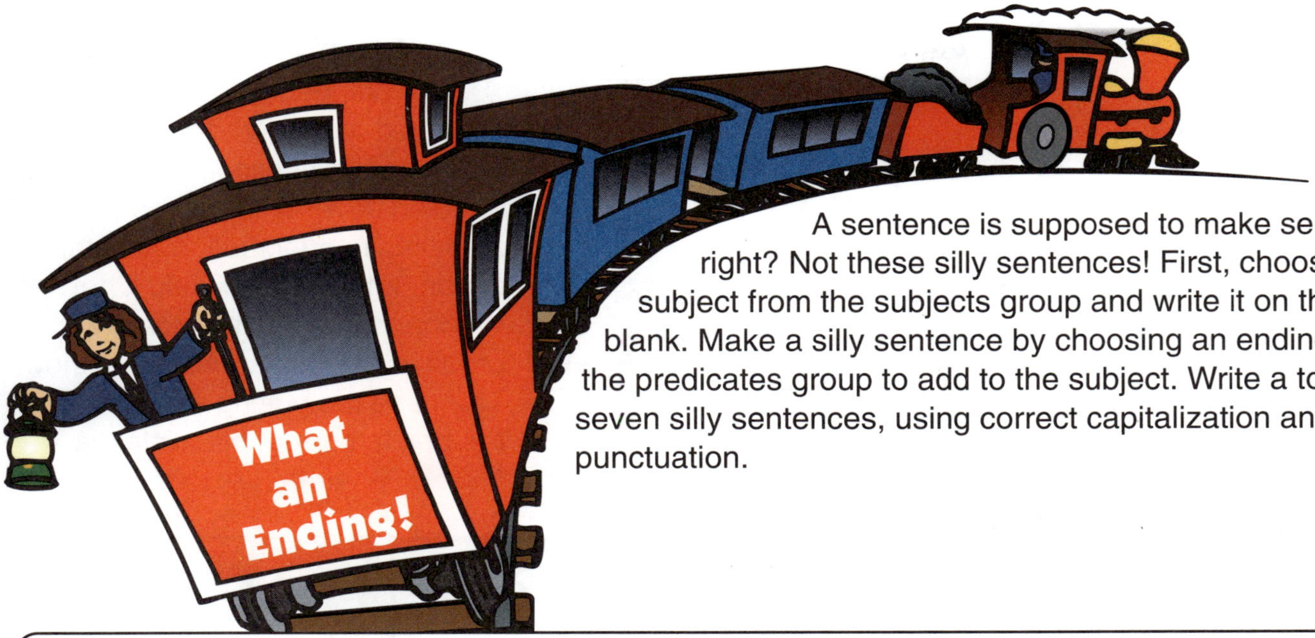

A sentence is supposed to make sense, right? Not these silly sentences! First, choose a subject from the subjects group and write it on the first blank. Make a silly sentence by choosing an ending from the predicates group to add to the subject. Write a total of seven silly sentences, using correct capitalization and punctuation.

Subjects	**Predicates**
all of principal smith's wastebaskets	was devastated by hurricane floyd
visitors to the white house	are needed to take care of washington school
seven custodians	were never sharpened
tourist sites in kentucky	is sponsoring a german festival in august
the lions club	hope to play in the world series
mom and dad	need to be emptied
one popular beach	want to meet the president and the first lady
three hundred write-right pencils	always brings us fresh georgia peaches
cousin carl	will fly on delta airlines to alaska
the pittsburgh pirates and the chicago cubs	will cross the atlantic ocean with their parents
jack and evelyn	are california grapes and maine lobster
my favorite summer foods	include churchill downs and mammoth cave

1. ______________________________

2. ______________________________

3. ______________________________

4. ______________________________

5. ______________________________

6. ______________________________

7. ______________________________

Try This: On another sheet of paper, match each subject with a predicate to create 12 sensible sentences. Capitalize and punctuate each sentence correctly.

Name ________________________________

Baking Up A Batch Of Editing Skills

Common Editing Marks		
symbol	**meaning**	**example**
(oval)	Check spelling.	The ice (creme) melted.
(circled dot)	Add a period.	She licked the lollipop⊙
^,	Add a comma.	The cake needed eggs^, butter, and milk.
∨'	Add an apostrophe.	The chef's hat is tall.
≡	Make capital.	the baker sliced the pie.
/	Make lowercase.	An ice Cream cone is tasty.
(close-up marks)	Close gap.	I ate the ca ke.

Chef Wannabe's goal is to be accepted at the School Of Dessert Science. His application has been rejected several times due to mistakes in punctuation, capitalization, and spelling. Help Chef Wannabe achieve his goal by proofreading his application below. Then use the editing symbols in the box to correct his mistakes.

School Of Dessert Science Application

Date: October 14 1999

Name: Chef I Wannabe

Address: 3515 Doughnut circle
Street

Hershey (City) Pa (State) 20202 (Zip)

Education		
	Name Of School	**Location Of School**
High School	Trifle High	Sweet Home oregon
College	University Of Sweetwater Station	Wyoming

References:

1. Chef Boy R. Dee (Name) — 232 Spaghetti boulevard (Address)
2. Mr D. Hines (Name) — 101 Cakeleaf Lane (Address)

Previous Experience:

1. I was the pie sli cer at miss Sweettree's bakery
2. last year i delivered frozen deserts two the local grocery stores.

Why do you want to attend the School Of Dessert Science?
Ive always wanted to bee a world famous dessert chef. I want to lern how to prepare delicious pies puddings, and Cakes.

Signature: *Chef Wannabe* **Date:** *October 14, 1999*

Reading Comprehension

The fourth-grade reading program is a challenging one. Having mastered the picture books enjoyed by second and third graders, fourth graders dive into chapter books. These longer books take maturing readers on new literary adventures and require much more effort on the reader's part. Fourth graders begin to look at character traits and motivation, the plot, and the setting, and they begin to make predictions about how problems will be solved.

Fourth-grade teachers encourage their students to select reading material on their individual reading levels to read during appropriate times. The student may have conferences with the teacher to discuss his independent reading, give a book report to the class, or complete a quiz on the book.

Your child's teacher will model and guide students through various reading experiences. *Guided reading experiences* focus on certain comprehension strategies through repeated readings and discussions. Fourth graders will be asked to explain material at a literal level: reading for sequence, details, or following directions. Fourth graders can also find the main idea in a selection, explain an author's choice of words, and draw conclusions. They can use context clues to understand words of increasing difficulty. Fourth graders also increase their vocabulary through interacting with media and Internet resources.

Your fourth grader will encounter the following reading comprehension skills:

- Reading for detail
- Finding the main idea
- Recalling sequence of events
- Determining cause and effect
- Using context clues
- Making inferences
- Drawing conclusions
- Reading charts and diagrams
- Analyzing character, setting, and plot
- Comparing and contrasting ideas

Reading on the Run

Encourage reading comprehension everywhere you go by questioning your child about signs, posters, billboards, videocassette covers, musical lyrics on the radio while you drive, etc. "Reading on the Run" is developmentally challenging for your fourth grader, and merely requires simple comprehension questions from you, such as "What was that billboard advertising?" or "What was the main point of that song we just heard?" You'll be surprised by how much confidence simple reading comprehension activities can build in your child.

Restaurant Reading

Here's another opportunity for real-life reading comprehension that ties in with your fourth grader's increasing appetite. Take time at fast-food restaurants, diners, pizzerias, and ice-cream parlors to question your child about the menu. Questions about fat content, pricing, side dishes, and other "restaurant reading" are easily answered by your child, and help develop reading-for-detail skills.

Comics Quiz

Your daily newspaper is a valuable tool for home-based learning. Serve up the comics with your child's breakfast each morning. Invest in a sticky pad of small sticky notes and have it handy. Then ask a simple question on a sticky note and place it next to your child's favorite cartoon strip. Questions can range in difficulty from "What food did Garfield eat in today's comics?" to "List the places the kids went in Family Circus today." This daily practice in comprehension will serve your child well in the chapter books he will soon be devouring at school!

Name ____

Follow The Signs To Sequencing

Directions: Read each group of sentences in each section below. Show the order of each section's events by writing a *1, 2,* or *3* in the blank before each sentence. Then follow the directions at the bottom of this page to decode a secret message.

A. ______ Jennifer washed her hands with the new soap.
______ Finally, Jennifer sat down to eat dinner with her family.
______ Then she dried her hands.

B. ______ First I asked for a hamburger and fries.
______ Then I changed my order to chicken fingers.
______ After I arrived at the restaurant, I looked at the menu to help me decide what to order.

C. ______ Jan bought a bag of candy.
______ Then she removed several pieces of candy and resealed the bag.
______ She opened the bag carefully.

D. ______ We have several events planned for the picnic.
______ Then we are going to have a relay race.
______ First we are going to have a pie-eating contest.

E. ______ Finally, he will put his clothes in the soapy water.
______ Next he will add some detergent.
______ James is going to turn on the water to wash his dirty clothes.

F. ______ We celebrate it by having cake and ice cream.
______ Jake's birthday is an important day for our family.
______ Afterwards we play games.

Now look back at the sentence in each section that you marked with a "1." Write the underlined words from those sentences in A–F order in the blanks below. If you marked your sentences correctly and recorded the underlined words in the right order, they will reveal a special message.

______________	______________	______________
A	B	C
______________	______________	______________
D	E	F

Name ______________________________

How Does Your Garden Grow?

Green-thumbed Gill wants to plant a garden in his yard. He read a gardening book for information, but got a little confused when he wrote his notes. Each sentence he wrote is false. Read the information below; then rewrite each sentence to make it true. Gill also did not write his notes in order. Place the steps in the correct order by writing the appropriate numeral (1–10) in the box to the left of each step.

Planting An Outdoor Garden

There are several steps you need to take when planting an outdoor garden. First, choose a site for your garden. Make sure the area is well drained. Plants won't grow well in soggy soil. The site should also receive the proper amount of light. Many flowers and most vegetables need a large amount of light to grow. Second, prepare the soil. Use a shovel to remove the grass and other plants that cover the site. Dig up the soil about 8 to 12 inches; then break it up by turning it over and over. Add fertilizer if it is needed. Then run a rake over the soil to make it smooth. Next choose the plants you want to grow. It helps to sketch a garden plan before planting to avoid making mistakes. Make sure the plants grow well in your climate. When you are ready to plant, space the seeds apart so the plants will have enough room to grow. Planting vegetables in straight rows makes them easier to care for. Flowers look attractive if they are planted in irregularly shaped groups. After your garden is planted, water it when the soil is dry.

☐ Use a shovel to remove the grass, but keep all other plants.
____

☐ Water your garden so much that the soil never gets dry.
____

☐ Add fertilizer after you have raked the soil smooth.
____

☐ Find a site with the proper sunlight.
____

☐ Dig up the soil no more than 8 inches.
____

☐ Plant vegetables in irregularly shaped groups so they can be cared for more easily.
____

☐ Choose a site where the water will keep the soil soggy.
____

☐ Space the seeds closely together so they don't grow all over the place.
____

☐ Choose plants that grow well in any climate.
____

☐ Draw a sketch of your garden after it grows to check for any mistakes.
____

Just The Facts, Please!

Directions: Read each statement below and decide whether it is a fact or an opinion. If the statement is a fact, color the eucalyptus leaf next to it green.

FACT: *a statement that is true and can be proven*
OPINION: *a statement of a personal belief or feeling that cannot be proven*

N 1. Koalas are the cutest animals of all.

I 2. The koala is a marsupial—or pouched—animal.

S 3. Koalas make their homes in trees.

M 4. Koalas seem to be happy animals.

A 5. Eucalyptus leaves do not have a good taste.

A 6. The average koala bear needs more than a pound of eucalyptus leaves every day.

E 7. Koala babies are funny-looking animals.

L 8. The word *koala* comes from the word *kaloine* which means “do not drink.”

O 9. Koalas are always very friendly.

U 10. The koala gets its water from the eucalyptus leaves that it eats.

A 11. Koalas sleep 18 to 20 hours a day.

R 12. The female koala raises her young alone.

T 13. Once a baby koala becomes too heavy for its mother’s pouch, she shifts the baby to her back.

C 14. Everyone who has a chance to see a koala will like this animal.

P 15. Koalas should be used as the next Olympic mascot.

A 16. Eucalyptus trees grow in Australia.

Unscramble the letters on the eucalyptus leaves that you colored to find out where koalas live. Spell this location in the blanks below.

______ ______ ______ ______ ______ ______ ______ ______ ______

Name________________

A Look Into The Future

Directions: Read each selection below carefully. Then write your prediction about what will happen next on the lines at the base of each crystal ball.

1. Jennifer has an important science test on the same day as the regional soccer finals. She practices soccer every evening until it is time to go to bed. She doesn't study her science notes. When Jennifer takes her science test, she...

PREDICTION:

2. Liz is getting ready to go walking with her friends, but she hasn't done any of her chores. As Liz goes to the door to meet her friends, her mother says...

PREDICTION:

3. Dave and Michelle want to visit a theme park next month, but they have no money. As they walk home from school, they see signs in a neighborhood store window about baby-sitting and cutting grass. Dave and Michelle...

PREDICTION:

4. Ray and Andrew know the rule that all scouts should stay with the group when hiking. But while walking through the canyon, the boys decide to take a shortcut to beat the rest of the pack back to camp. As the sun begins to set, they see no sign of their camp. The boys...

PREDICTION:

5. Sharon arrived on time for her 1:00 hair appointment. Carolyn—the hairdresser—rolled Sharon's hair and applied the perming solution. Then Carolyn got an unexpected phone call and did not return to check on Sharon as scheduled. When Carolyn returned, Sharon's hair...

PREDICTION:

Stormy Effects

Storms are known for their terrible effects—on both people and property. See if you can complete the following cause-and-effect statements about storms. Read each cause; then choose a matching effect from the box and write it on the blank. Use encyclopedias, almanacs, your science textbook, and other resources to help you. The first one has been done for you.

Causes

1. Since the new hurricane was the fourth of the season, *it was named David.*
2. The cloud was tall, dark, and anvil-shaped, ______
3. Because we had a blizzard warning, ______
4. Since the storm was called a *typhoon,* ______
5. Storm surges were predicted when the hurricane hit the coast, ______
6. Because thunderstorms pump lots of hot air from the earth's surface high into the air, ______
7. Since we have no basement, ______
8. Because Hugo was such a terrible hurricane, ______
9. Whenever I hear thunder, ______
10. We spotted a tornado while driving in a car, ______
11. Since the tornado was classified as an F-5, ______
12. There were 15 seconds between when I saw lightning and then heard thunder, ______

Effects

- we made sure we had blankets and food in the car before driving to town.
- they are called earth's "air-conditioning system."
- I know there has been lightning.
- so I knew the storm was three miles away.
- it was named *David.*
- so we evacuated the island.
- that name will never be used again.
- we knew houses and cars had been blown away.
- so we knew it was a cumulonimbus cloud.
- my family gathers in the bathroom in the center of our house during a tornado warning.
- so we stopped and took cover in a deep ditch.
- I knew that it wasn't located in the United States.

Name ______________________________ Reading comprehension: cause and effect

Picture Perfect

Directions: Look at the pictures below. Match them by drawing a line connecting them. Bring these pictures depicting cause and effect to life using your very own words. Write the cause and the effect.

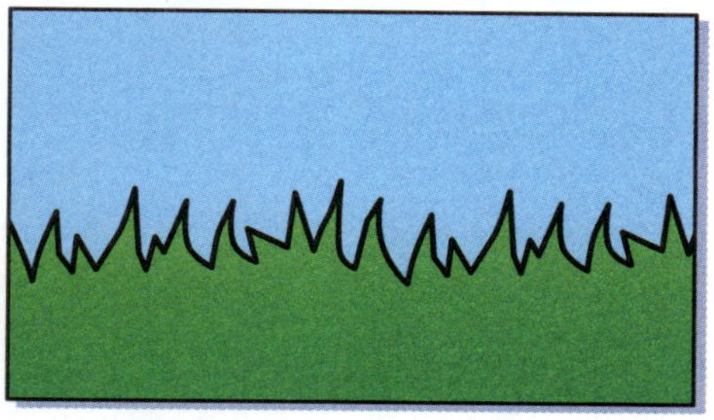

Name________________________________

Jordan's Tale

Michael Jordan is an incredible athlete. He has a tremendous amount of courage combined with an undying will. Because of these traits, and his tremendous talent, he is one of the best basketball players that has ever lived.

Michael won Rookie of the Year in 1984 in the NBA draft. He was then chosen by the Chicago Bulls. Michael played for 14 years until he announced his retirement in October 1993. He felt he had nothing more to prove in basketball. He also said that the media had made his private life intolerable. After a while, Michael missed competing, so he went back to his original sport, baseball, for a short time. He returned to basketball, however, on March 19, 1995. It took him time to get back up to speed after his 21-month absence. From 1995 to 1997, the Chicago Bulls won 171 games and lost only 30. Michael was then 35 and was still considered to be in his prime when most players would have been past theirs. He is one athlete you can't help but admire!

Directions: Read the following statements. Mark a "T" next to the number if the statement is true and an "F" if it is false. If the statement is false, correct it to make it true.

1. ______ Michael Jordan is an unbelievable athlete.

   ____

2. ______ Michael won Rookie of the Year in 1982 in high school.

   ____

3. ______ Michael played for 14 years and felt he still had to prove himself.

   ____

4. ______ He said that the media had made his life intolerable.

   ____

5. ______ Michael then played baseball for a short time.

   ____

6. ______ Michael returned to basketball on March 19, 1993.

   ____

7. ______ It took no time at all to get back up to speed.

   ____

8. ______ Michael didn't win that many games for the Chicago Bulls, even though he was a great player.

   ____

   ____

Name ______________________________

Tools Of The Time

Throughout time people have invented tools to help make life easier. Complete the activity below to learn more about some colonial conveniences.

Directions:

1. Look at each tool pictured and read its name.
2. Then use the clues to match each tool to its correct description.
3. Write the name of each tool in the box beside its matching description.

	1. This portable tool was used during colder months. It was a pierced metal box often mounted on wooden legs. A colonist placed hot coals inside, then put his feet on top of it to keep warm.		5. Corn was a staple of the colonial diet. Colonists used this bowl and stick to grind corn into flour. It was similar to the tool used by pharmacists to grind medication.
	2. This tool was used to gather wool for spinning. It was made of thin rectangular boards with handles. Each board had a leather strip filled with wire teeth. The wool was collected by brushing the tool across a sheep, then scraping the boards together to roll the wool into balls.		6. Colonists took the chill out of a cold bed with the help of this tool. It was a circular metal pan with a long wooden handle. The pan was filled with coals from the fire, then moved quickly between the bed's covers to heat them up.
	3. This tool helped colonists make cloth for clothing. A foot pedal was used to turn a wheel that spun the wool or flax to be made into cloth.		7. This tool was an iron rack on stilts or legs. A colonist would place bread in the rack, then use its long handle to put it near the fire. The stilts kept it just above the hot coals.
	4. This tool was a wooden container with a long handle. Butter was made by pumping cream up and down in it.		8. This tool was used for light. A colonist filled its container with grease or oil, then lighted the wick placed in its small spout. Its hook and chain allowed it to be hung where needed.

wooden churn

warming pan

toasting rack

wool cards

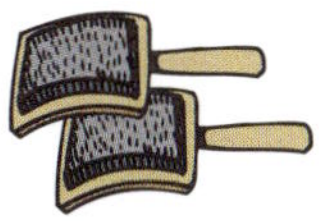

foot stove

corn pestle

spinning wheel

Betty lamp

Name____

Extra! Extra! Read All About It!

Here's the scoop! Each paragraph below tells something about newspapers and how they are made. Read each paragraph to find the meaning of its headline. Next write the meaning of that headline on the lines below each paragraph. Then underline the clues in each paragraph that helped you understand each headline's meaning.

1.

Newsprint

A newspaper tells about and comments on the news. Sixty million copies of daily newspapers are circulated throughout the United States every day. Newspapers are printed on newsprint, a coarse paper made from wood pulp.

____

____

____

____

____

2.

Tabloid

The two most common sizes of newspapers are standard and tabloid. A standard-sized newspaper measures about 13 x 21 1/2 inches. A tabloid's pages are about half the size of a standard newspaper's pages. Tabloids report the news with lots of pictures, larger headlines, and shorter articles.

____

____

____

____

____

3.

Beat Reporters

Newspapers use different kinds of reporters. General reporters cover any story to which they are assigned. Reporters who cover news in one particular location or about one particular subject are called beat reporters. For example, a beat reporter may report only the news from city hall or about education.

____

____

____

____

____

4.

Lead

Reporters start each news story with a lead—the first paragraph, which contains important facts. The reporter then completes the story with details that tell who, what, when, where, why, and/or how.

____

____

____

____

____

5.

Copy Editor

A reporter's completed story is taken to someone who checks it for accuracy and writes a headline for it. This person may change some words to make the article easier to understand or cut some information if the story is too long. The person responsible for this job is called a copy editor.

____

____

____

____

____

6.

Layout

Artists create a layout—or sketch—of each newspaper page. Most newspaper artists are able to quickly plan where each story, picture, and advertisement will be placed on a page by using computers.

____

____

____

____

____

Name ______________________________ Context clues

Mammoth: World's Greatest Cave

It's been the home of a hospital for **tuberculosis** patients. It's been the setting for weddings, picnics, plays, and concerts. In the mid-1800s, a visitor described Kentucky's Mammoth Cave as "nothing but darkness, silence, **immensity.**"

Parts of this underground **labyrinth** were discovered by Indians about 4,000 years ago. Human mummies, early tools, and bits of clothing have been found in the cave. All were well **preserved.** Why? The temperature inside the cave is always 54° Fahrenheit. The humidity is low and there is no natural light.

By the time of the War of 1812, the property had changed **hands** several times. In 1812, a **rich** supply of **saltpeter** was found near the cave's opening. Saltpeter was used in making matches, gunpowder, and explosives. Business was soon **thriving** for the cave owners. During the war, they supplied saltpeter for 200 tons of gunpowder.

Black slaves worked the mines in Mammoth Cave during the war. Some **ventured** into the **eerie channels** beyond the mines. Stephen Bishop, a 17-year-old slave, became the cave's first sight-seeing guide. Bishop was famous for his **daring** explorations and knowledge of the cave's inner **recesses.** He and two slave guides who **succeeded** him discovered many of the cave's secrets. They found underground lakes and rivers.

Eyeless fish swim in the rivers. Blind shrimp and crayfish **grope** their way to food. Blind beetles and crickets climb the cave walls. These creatures' sensitive bodies make up for their lack of the sense of sight.

The still-changing passages in Mammoth Cave are now on five different levels. They **extend** as deep as several hundred feet. Mammoth Cave may be as much as 500 miles long! The 330 miles that have been mapped so far make it the longest cave in the world.

Since 1941, Mammoth Cave has been part of the National Park Service. A variety of breathtaking tours are available to visitors—from a one-and-a-half-hour tour for the disabled to the six-hour Wild Cave tour for the **hardy.**

Directions: Match each boldface word in the article with its definition below. Three definitions will not be used. Mark an *X* in the blank of a definition that is not used.

1. bold ____________
2. kept from decomposing ____________
3. wealthy ____________
4. to feel about blindly for something ____________
5. prospering ____________
6. potassium nitrate ____________
7. passageways ____________
8. very productive ____________
9. proceeded in the face of danger ____________
10. owners ____________
11. to stretch forth ____________
12. vigorous ____________
13. hidden or secret places ____________
14. came next after another ____________
15. a disease that affects the lungs ____________
16. greatness in size ____________
17. maze ____________
18. periods of rest from schoolwork ____________
19. had a favorable or desired outcome ____________
20. mysterious and strange ____________

Name ______________________

Super Chris!

Christopher Reeve is best known for playing Superman in a series of movies. As Superman, he was a superhero who could fly and achieve great feats. As a man, he also accomplishes great things.

Several years ago, Christopher fell from his horse during a riding show. He broke his spinal cord and is now paralyzed from the neck down. After a lot of the sadness, frustration, and anger had passed, he decided to be a voice for paralyzed people in the United States. He has spoken out for medical research to help quadriplegics. He says that one of his biggest goals is to hug his son again. He believes that day will come.

Despite his physical limitations, he continues to make public appearances, direct movies, and act. Christopher Reeve continues to be an example to us all. He is perhaps more of a Superman now than he ever was in the movies!

Directions: Answer the following questions. Use facts from the passage, as well as knowledge you already have, to help you.

1. What can you infer about Christopher Reeve's character?

____

2. In what ways does Christopher show courage?

____

3. What examples from the story make you think that Christopher isn't a quitter?

____

4. Do you think Christopher lets his paralysis hold him back? Explain your answer.

____

5. Do you think Christopher will continue fighting to get well?

____

6. Has Christopher been a good role model? Explain.

____

____

____

Name ____________________

Aboard Columbus's Ships

The most important tools of the trade for Christopher Columbus were his ships. The *Santa María* was his *flagship,* the ship carrying the admiral. It was followed by the *Niña* and the *Pinta.* The diagram of the ship below is similar to the three ships that Columbus took on his voyage to the New World. Use the description of each ship part below to help you label each numbered item on the diagram. When you are finished, use colored pencils to color your ship. Place a small X on the ship where you think the sailors slept while on the ship.

stern: the rear part of a ship, beginning where the sides curve inward
bow: the front end of a ship
keel: the main wooden or steel piece that extends the whole length of the bottom of a ship
mainmast: the largest mast of a ship (a mast is a long pole set upright on a ship)
mizzenmast: the mast nearest the stern
crow's nest: a small, enclosed platform for the lookout, near the top of a ship's mast
mainsail: the largest sail of a ship located on the mainmast
shrouds: a series of ropes that help support the mast
yard: a long wooden pole, hoisted up the mast, to which the sail is attached
rudder: a flat, movable piece of wood or metal at the rear end of a ship, by which it is steered
anchor: a shaped piece of metal attached to a rope or chain and used to hold a ship in place

1. ____________________
2. ____________________
3. ____________________
4. ____________________
5. ____________________
6. ____________________
7. ____________________
8. ____________________
9. ____________________
10. ____________________
11. ____________________

Name ____

The Ways Of The Wind

Young Francis Beaufort joined the British Royal Navy and went to sea when he was only 12 years old. While at sea, he studied the ways of the wind. In 1805 he made a scale to determine the wind speed by looking at things around him—trees, flags, smoke, and so on. This scale is known today as the Beaufort scale, and sailors, meteorologists, and others continue to rely on it.

Directions: The table below includes the information from the Beaufort scale. Use the table to answer the questions below.

BEAUFORT SCALE

Beaufort Number	Name Of Wind	Signs/Description	Wind Speed/mph
0	calm	calm; smoke rises vertically	<1
1	light air	smoke drifts, indicating wind direction	1–3
2	light breeze	wind felt on face; leaves rustle; flags stir	4–7
3	gentle breeze	leaves and small twigs in constant motion	8–12
4	moderate breeze	small branches move; wind raises dust and loose paper	13–18
5	fresh breeze	small-leaved trees begin to sway; crested wavelets form on inland water	19–24
6	strong breeze	overhead wires whistle; umbrellas difficult to control; large branches move	25–31
7	moderate gale or near gale	whole trees sway; walking against wind is difficult	32–38
8	fresh gale or gale	twigs break off trees; moving cars veer	39–46
9	strong gale	slight structural damage occurs, such as signs and antennas blown down	47–54
10	whole gale or storm	trees uprooted; considerable structural damage occurs	55–63
11	storm or violent storm	widespread damage occurs	64–74
12	hurricane	widespread damage occurs	>74

1. What is the name of the wind that has the Beaufort number of 7? ____________________
2. Describe a wind that has a speed of 36 mph. ____________________
   ____
3. What is the speed of a wind that causes twigs to break off trees? ____________________
4. Name the winds that are weaker than a gentle breeze. ____________________
   ____
5. Calculate the difference between the strongest speed of wind 2 and the strongest speed of wind 9. ____________________
6. What are the signs of a strong gale? ____________________
   ____
7. What is the name of the wind that causes smoke to rise vertically? ____________________
8. Find the difference between the weakest and strongest speeds of a fresh breeze.
   ____
9. Name the winds that are stronger than a fresh gale. ____________________
   ____
10. How fast must the wind be blowing in order for a hurricane to occur? ____________________

Name ______________________________

Chill Check

Brrrrrrr! It's cold, and this chart will tell you exactly how cold! If you know the outside air temperature and the speed of the wind, you can use the chart below to find out the *wind chill factor.* The wind chill factor tells what the temperature really feels like. For example, if the temperature is 5°F and wind is blowing at 20 mph, it will seem like it's –31°F. The temperature of –31°F is the wind chill factor (wcf) for those conditions.

Study the chart below as you answer questions 1–10:

Wind Chill Factors
thermometer reading in degrees Fahrenheit

Wind speed (mph)	35	30	25	20	15	10	5	0	–5	–10	–15	–20	–25
5	33	27	21	19	12	7	0	–5	–10	–15	–21	–26	–31
10	22	16	10	3	–3	–9	–15	–22	–27	–34	–40	–46	–52
15	16	9	2	–5	–11	–18	–25	–31	–38	–45	–51	–58	–65
20	12	4	–3	–10	–17	–24	–31	–39	–46	–53	–60	–67	–74
25	8	1	–7	–15	–22	–29	–36	–44	–51	–59	–66	–74	–81
30	6	–2	–10	–18	–25	–33	–41	–49	–56	–64	–71	–79	–86
35	4	–4	–12	–20	–27	–35	–43	–52	–58	–67	–74	–82	–89
40	3	–5	–13	–21	–29	–37	–45	–53	–60	–69	–76	–84	–92

Remember: As minus numbers (–5, –29, –84) get larger, the temperature becomes colder. In this set, –84°F is the coldest temperature.

1. If the wind speed is 15 mph and the temperature is 10°F, what is the wind chill factor?
   ____
2. At that same temperature (10°F), by how many degrees does the wcf change if the wind speed increases by 5 mph? ______________________
3. What is the wind chill factor for a temperature of –25°F and a wind speed of 30 mph?
   ____
4. What is the wcf for a temperature of 0°F and a wind speed of 40 mph? ______________
5. At that same temperature (0°F), what is the change in the wcf if the wind speed decreases by 10 mph? ______________________
6. The temperature is –10°F and the wcf is –45°F. What is the wind speed? ____________
7. The wind speed is 20 mph and the wcf is –10°F. What is the temperature? ____________
8. Which gives the lower (colder) wcf: –5°F with 30 mph winds or –15°F with 10 mph winds?
   ____
9. Which gives the highest (warmest) wcf: 10°F with 30 mph winds, –5°F with 15 mph winds, or –25°F with 5 mph winds? ______________________
10. Find two different pairs of temperatures and wind speeds that have the same wcf: ________
    ____

Wave Of Immigration

Over 37 million immigrants entered the United States between 1901 and 1990. More than 12 million immigrants found their way to the United States by first stopping off at Ellis Island. For over 60 years, Ellis Island served as a reception center for immigrants entering the United States in search of a better life.

Directions: Use the information in the graph below to answer questions about immigration to the United States.

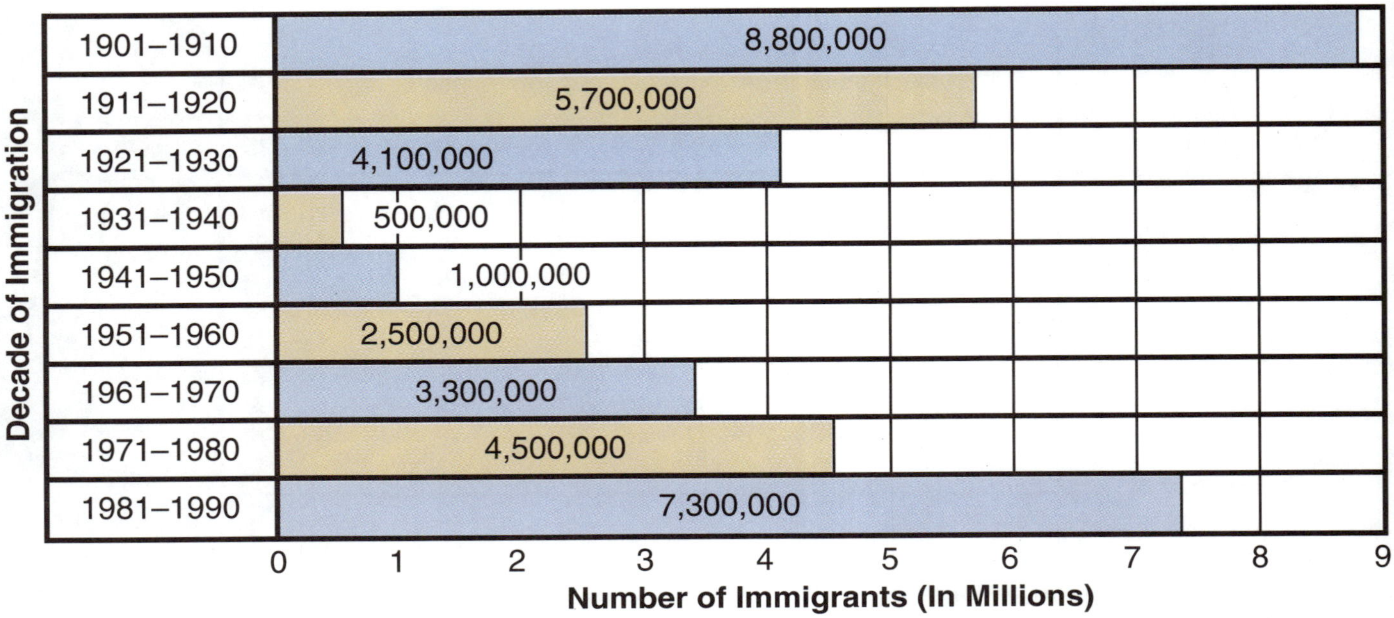

1. The greatest number of immigrants came to the United States during what decade?

 ____

2. During what decade did the least number of immigrants come to the United States?

 ____

3. What major economic event in the United States might help account for the low number of immigrants during this decade? ______________________

4. The second lowest number of immigrants entered the United States during what decade?

 ____

5. How many more immigrants came to the United States from 1901–1910 than from 1911–1920? ______________________

6. Has the number of immigrants coming to the United States increased or decreased since 1951–1960? ______________________

7. What decade had the greatest increase in immigrants over the one before it?

 ____

8. What decade had the greatest decrease in immigrants from the decade before it?

 ____

Try This: Use the information provided to determine the average number of immigrants entering the United States per year from 1901–1990.

Name ______________________________

High Fliers

Ever wonder what the pioneers of aviation were really like? To find out, read each description below; then circle the best word that describes the character trait being shown by these pilots and inventors.

1. In 1782, Joseph and Etienne Montgolfier of France noticed that smoke rises, so they tried filling a small silk bag with smoke from a fire and created the first hot-air balloon.
   a. reliable
   b. observant
   c. careful

2. In the early 1800s, Sir George Cayley was the first to realize that a properly shaped wing was the key to making an airplane that would fly. He published his principles of aerodynamics, which would revolutionize flight almost 100 years later.
   a. brilliant
   b. joyful
   c. stubborn

3. Otto Lilienthal made over 2,000 glider flight attempts in an effort to learn more about flight.
   a. dependable
   b. persistent
   c. considerate

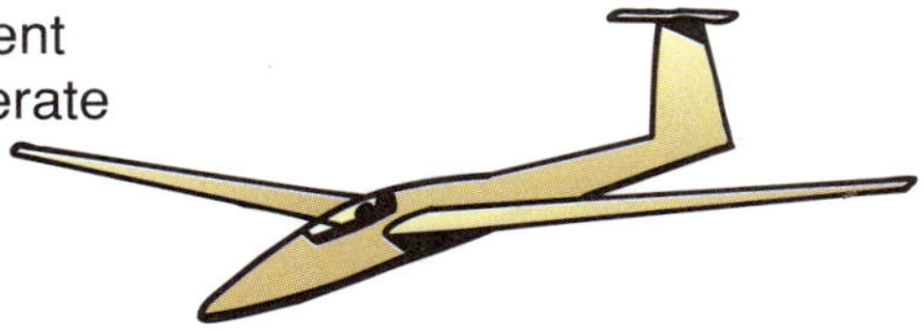

4. The Wright brothers pooled their talents and worked together to invent the first manned plane, which flew on December 17, 1903.
   a. kind
   b. careless
   c. cooperative

5. Glenn Curtiss thought of putting pontoons on a plane so it could take off and land in the water. He made the first seaplane in 1910.
   a. creative
   b. courteous
   c. sneaky

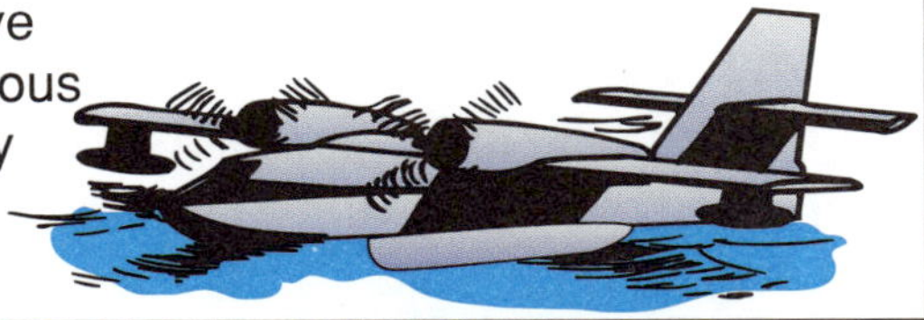

6. Igor Sikorsky of Russia traveled several times to Paris seeking information on flight and engines. His company built more than 200 planes between 1926 and 1942 and also made 131 helicopters by the end of World War II.
   a. cheerful
   b. proud
   c. hardworking

7. Charles Lindbergh, in his plane *The Spirit of St. Louis,* fought fog, clouds, ice on his wings, and extreme tiredness to make the first non-stop Atlantic Ocean solo flight from New York City to Paris in 1927. It took him over 33 hours.
   a. smart
   b. ignorant
   c. determined

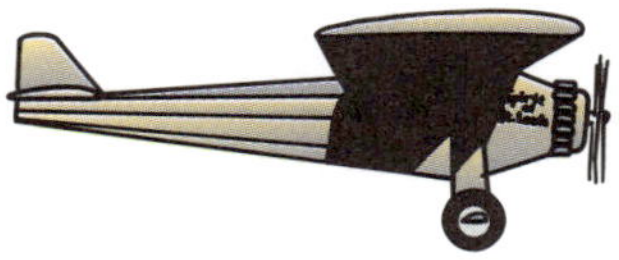

8. Amelia Earhart was the first woman to fly many epic flights, such as flying solo across the Atlantic. She wanted to be the first woman to fly around the world in 1937, but her plane disappeared midflight.
   a. considerate
   b. joyful
   c. daring

9. Chuck Yeager was the first to fly faster than the speed of sound, even though other aircraft had broken apart when approaching high speeds in other test flights.
   a. careless
   b. brave
   c. creative

10. The U.S. Air Force and Northrop Grumman unveiled a special type of plane in 1988. This plane could travel secretly past enemy sites at night.
    a. shy
    b. inventive
    c. confident

Wilma Rudolph: Gold Olympian

"You gain strength, courage, and confidence by every experience in which you stop to look fear in the face. You must do the thing which you think you cannot do."

On June 23, 1940, a tiny baby was born to Blanche and Ed Rudolph. She weighed only four and a half pounds! Medical care was quite different then. Many infants died at birth—so the odds were against her living. Wilma's parents were poor. They could not pay for expensive hospital care. Mr. Rudolph worked as a railroad porter and handyman. Mrs. Rudolph did light housekeeping and sewing for other families. Wilma was their 20th child. Would the tiny tot survive? Yes! The family rejoiced.

Children born **prematurely** are often sickly. Wilma seemed to come down with one childhood disease after another. Diseases such as *measles* and *mumps* can be prevented today. But, there were no vaccinations then. One day Wilma became very ill. Again the Rudolphs feared for her life. Again Wilma survived. However, this illness left her crippled. Wilma was **diagnosed** with *polio.*

Polio is a disease that attacks the central nervous system. It affects the body's muscles, causing a loss of muscle control. The doctors told Mrs. Rudolph that her daughter would never walk again. Wilma's mother set out to prove the doctors wrong.

Wilma and her mother began a series of trips to Meharry Medical College in Nashville, Tennessee. It was located about 50 miles away. There young Wilma received massages and water therapy. Each day Wilma did exercises to rebuild strength in her leg. It would have been easy to just give up, but the Rudolphs **persisted.**

At the age of 11, Wilma's leg brace was removed. She could walk again! She could join in games with all the other children. Wilma loved the feel of running. Her tall frame made her very fast. Others began to notice her natural athletic ability.

Wilma put her energy into training for track. She wanted to be the best. She was **resolute.** There was no stopping Wilma Rudolph. She earned the nickname Skeeter because she was always buzzing around. In 1956 Wilma became the youngest member of the American Olympic team. At the age of 16 she won a bronze medal. Four years later Wilma returned to the Olympics. This time she became the first American woman to win three gold medals. It was a proud moment for Wilma and the United States of America.

Wilma had struggled to overcome poverty, illness, and **racism.** She became a victor. She married and had children. Wilma spent her remaining years working as a teacher and coach. In 1977 she published her autobiography. Wilma Rudolph proved by her example how anything is possible. She was presented the first National Sports Award by President Bill Clinton in 1993. She died in 1994 at the age of 54. Wilma Rudolph was a true champion.

Name ______________________________ Comprehension: recalling details

Wilma Rudolph: Gold Olympian

Answer the following items. Use another sheet of paper if you need more space.

1. How is medical care in the 1990s better than that of the 1940s? ______________________________

____

____

2. What is *polio?* ______________________________

____

3. What physical challenge did Wilma overcome? ______________________________

____

4. How do you think Wilma's early life shaped her personality? ______________________________

____

5. Why was Wilma given the nickname Skeeter? ______________________________

____

6. Think about Wilma's quote. What fears do you think she faced in her life? What fears would you like to overcome? ______________________________

____

____

7. What did Wilma achieve at the 1960 Olympics? ______________________________

____

8. Define *prematurely, diagnosed, persisted, resolute,* and *racism* as they are used in the article.

____

____

____

9. Which sports hero do you most admire? Explain. ______________________________

____

10. On a separate sheet of paper, describe a goal that is important to you. Then tell what you can do to achieve it.

Carl Sagan: Author And Astronomer

"I believe our future depends on how well we know this cosmos in which we float like a mote of dust in the morning sky."

The young boy gazed up at the night sky. The stars seemed so different from the sun and moon. Why? "I'll find out for myself," he thought. Carl rode the streetcar to the Brooklyn branch of the public library. He asked for a book about stars. He read it right there. He learned that the stars are just like our sun. "The universe must be much bigger than I ever imagined," Carl thought.

Carl's interest in astronomy grew. His mom and dad encouraged him to read and learn more. By the age of eight, Carl decided there must be life on other planets. Books written by Jules Verne and H. G. Wells **fired** his imagination. Carl told his grandfather he wanted to become an astronomer. "Fine," his grandfather replied, "but how will you make a living?" Carl's high-school teacher told him about a famous astronomer who was paid! Carl was encouraged. He would not have to choose between studying the stars and earning a living.

Carl graduated with honors from high school. He received a scholarship from the University of Chicago. Enrico Fermi, a great physicist, and Harold Urey, a noted chemist, both taught there. Carl studied under these Nobel Prize winners. He also spent one summer as a research assistant for H. J. Muller. Muller had also won a Nobel Prize. He had discovered that X rays cause changes in genes.

Carl earned college degrees in physics and astronomy. He researched the conditions on Venus and Mars. Carl began a lifelong **quest** to find life beyond Earth. He also played an important part in the U.S. spacecraft probes to the planets.

But Carl was bothered by the public's lack of interest in space. He wondered what he could do. The result was the award-winning "Cosmos" television series. Carl hosted each of the 13 programs. He discussed topics such as comets, meteorites, and life on other planets. "Cosmos" was the most-watched series in public-television history. His book *Cosmos* was the best-selling science book ever published in the English language!

Carl continued to publish articles and books. He wrote another book titled *The Dragons Of Eden.* It won a Pulitzer Prize. Carl wrote an article about the effects that nuclear war would have on Earth. His theory of nuclear winter became a hotly debated topic. He believed a nuclear war would cause widespread cold and dark.

Carl Sagan continued to promote science education until his death in 1996. He dreamed of finding **extraterrestrial** life. However, he said that not finding life anywhere else makes life on our planet even more rare and precious.

Name ______________________________

Carl Sagan: Author And Astronomer

1. Reread the beginning quote. What does Carl compare the earth to? Why is this a good comparison? ______________________________

2. Describe Carl as a young boy. ______________________________

3. How did Carl pursue his interest in the stars? ______________________________

4. Define *fired, quest,* and *extraterrestrial* as they are used in the article. ______________________________

5. Carl read science fiction written by which two authors? ______________________________

   Describe your favorite science-fiction book, TV show, or movie. ______________________________

6. Carl studied biology, chemistry, history, and physics. How do you think this knowledge helped him be a better astronomer? ______________________________

7. Carl wanted to find extraterrestrial life. Do you think there is life elsewhere in the universe? Explain. ______________________________

8. "Cosmos" covered many fascinating fields of study. Number the following 1–9 in order by what you find most interesting (1 = *most* interesting): ___astronomy ___biology ___botany ___chemistry ___embryology ___ geology ___meteorology ___paleontology ___zoology

9. Two new asteroids were discovered and named for Carl Sagan and his wife, Ann Druyan. Suppose you discovered a new asteroid. What would you name it and why? ______________________________

10. What is a *theory?* Design a poster showing your own theory about why the dinosaurs disappeared. ______________________________

Mother Teresa Of Calcutta (1910–1997)

The small woman in the white **sari** climbed the platform. Her face was burned brown from many years in the hot sun of India. "I am grateful to receive the Nobel," she said. The Nobel Peace Prize is perhaps the greatest honor a person can receive. Mother Teresa, a Catholic nun, **devoted** many years of her life to helping the poor. Her story is an inspiring one.

Mother Teresa's real name was Agnes Bojaxhiu (pronounced *Boy-ya-jee-oo*). She was born in an area of Yugoslavia that is now called Macedonia. She came from a deeply religious family. Agnes liked to go to church to pray and sing. When Agnes was nine, her father died. Mrs. Bojaxhiu worked hard to support her three children by sewing for others. But still, she never forgot those who were less fortunate.

Young Agnes felt God had something special planned for her. She prayed and talked to her mother and sister about it. Then the decision was made. She would become a **missionary** in India. It was hard leaving her family, friends, and homeland, yet she knew she must. Agnes joined a **convent** called Loreto Abbey. There she learned to speak English and was trained in religious life. She also took a new name, *Sister Teresa.*

Teresa was later sent to the city of Calcutta as a teacher. Near the school was one of the greatest **slums** in the city. Teresa could not close her eyes to this. Who would help care for the poor who were living in the streets? Then one day she heard God's voice again. His message was clear. She had to leave the convent to live with and serve the poorest of the poor.

Teresa received some medical training so that she could help care for the people living in the slums. But was one person going to make a difference? Yes! She began a new religious community called the *Missionaries of Charity* and became known as *Mother Teresa.* Her community provided food for the needy and ran hospitals, schools, and shelters for the poor. Others soon joined her mission. Many were her former students.

Mother Teresa said, "Calcutta can be found all over the world if you have eyes to see." She then began Missionaries of Charity in Latin America, the United States, Asia, Africa, and other areas. Mother Teresa became a role model for many people. She knew that she alone could not erase the effects of poverty, but she could help. Her life showed that one person can truly make a difference in the lives of others!

Name______________________________________ Comprehension: recalling details

Mother Teresa Of Calcutta (1910–1997)

Answer the following items. Use another sheet of paper if you need more space.

1. Circle the letter of the best title for this article.
   A. Life In India
   B. A Missionary To The Poor
   C. The Nobel Peace Prize
   D. Calcutta—A City In India

2. Define *sari, devoted, missionary, convent,* and *slums* as they are used in the article.

3. What honor did Mother Teresa receive for her work?

4. How do you think Mother Teresa's early experiences influenced her later life?

5. How did Mother Teresa's life change after she decided to become a missionary to India?

6. What did Mother Teresa feel that God wanted her to do?

7. What new religious community did Mother Teresa begin and what did it do for others?

8. What do you think Mother Teresa meant when she said, "Calcutta can be found all over the world if you have eyes to see"?

Gloria Estefan: Singer And Entertainer

"Get on your feet!
Get up and make it happen!
Get on your feet!
Stand up and take some action!"

Gloria Estefan is a ball of energy as she performs her big hit. The audience applauds wildly. Then the tempo changes. Gloria now croons the words to a ballad titled "Don't Wanna Lose You." This song has climbed to number one on U.S. music charts. People everywhere love Estefan's unique blend of music. It combines the sounds of her native Cuba with pop music. Gloria's life has been a blending of two cultures—Hispanic and American.

Gloria Maria Fajardo was born on September 1, 1957, in Havana, Cuba. Her parents fled Cuba after Fidel Castro came into power. Mr. Fajardo always hoped to return to Cuba. He joined other exiles in the 1961 Bay of Pigs invasion of Cuba. They had hoped to oust the new government, but the operation was a failure. Mr. Fajardo was captured and jailed. A year and a half later the family was reunited in Miami, Florida.

Gloria's dad then entered the U.S. Army. The family moved frequently. Gloria recalls the loneliness she felt being the only Latina in her class at school. She began to use music to help her overcome the sadness of feeling out of place. She spent countless hours playing her guitar. Gloria later had to care for her father after he returned from Vietnam. He had been badly poisoned by a chemical called Agent Orange.

When Gloria was 17 years old, she sang at a wedding. Emilio Estefan heard her. He asked Gloria to join his band. Soon Gloria was performing regularly with the Miami Sound Machine. She had no idea stardom was ahead. She continued in school and graduated from the University of Miami in 1978. That same year she married Emilio. Emilio had also immigrated from Cuba.

The band's first big break came when it landed a major recording contract. It released several Spanish albums. Its popularity soared in Latin American countries. Then in 1984 the band made a crossover song. "Dr. Beat," sung in English, began climbing America's pop charts. The Cuban-influenced sound was a hit in America.

In the late 1980s, Estefan began a solo career. Some of her hit songs have included "Can't Stay Away From You" and "Coming Out Of The Dark." In 1990 tragedy struck. Gloria's tour bus was involved in a terrible accident. Her back was broken! She had to undergo dangerous surgery. Would she ever be able to perform her rousing dance numbers again? With a lot of courage and determination, Estefan recovered. In 1991 she recorded a popular album called *Into The Light*. In 1994 she gave birth to Emily, her second child. Her first child, son Nayib, was born in 1980.

Gloria Estefan has accomplished many great things. She has won many music awards. She and her husband now have their own private record label. Gloria has also "given something back" to the country that gave her family refuge. She raised millions of dollars to help the victims of Hurricane Andrew.

Gloria's music has brought a rich diversity to America's pop music world. She has been a bridge between two cultures.

Name ______________________________ Comprehension, critical thinking, drawing conclusions

Gloria Estefan: Singer And Entertainer

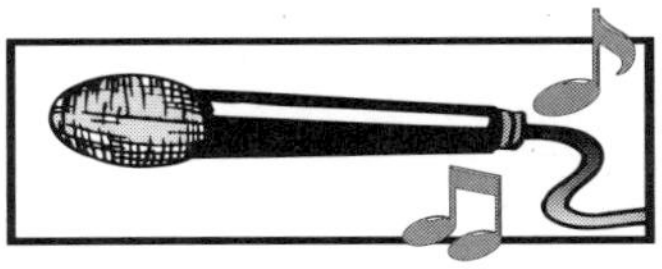

Complete the following. Use another sheet of paper if you need more space.

1. Why did Estefan and her parents immigrate to the United States? ______________________________

2. Why did Estefan often feel "out of place" growing up? ______________________________

3. Define the following words: *tempo, croons, native,* and *exiles.* ______________________________

4. Why is Estefan's music often thought of as "crossover" music? ______________________________

5. Many refugees want to enter the United States each year. Why do you think this is so? ______________________________

6. Estefan's musical gifts have made her a superstar. What special gifts and talents do you have? ______________________________

7. Locate Miami on a map. Why do you think it has developed into a center of Cuban culture? ______________________________

8. Choose one of these words: *refugee, Latina, soloist,* or *Hispanic.* Explain how it describes Gloria. ______________________________

9. Estefan hopes that her music can be used to bring people together. What are some other ways people from different ethnic groups can be united? ______________________________

10. How much time do you spend listening to the radio? To CDs? Who are your favorite artists? How would you describe their styles? ______________________________

General Colin Powell
American Hero

"Trust me," said the general during one of his many newscasts. His manner was calm and confident. Throughout the Persian Gulf War, General Colin Powell appeared on television many times. He knew it was important for the American people to be well **informed** about the war's progress. After only 42 days, the fighting came to an end. The general's mission had been a success! Later that year, President George Bush awarded Colin the Medal of Freedom for leading our country through a difficult time.

Colin Luther Powell was born on April 5, 1937, in Harlem, a black community in New York City. His parents moved there from Jamaica in search of a better life. Colin's parents worked very hard to provide for their family, but still found time for him and his sister. Work and family were the two most important things to the Powells.

When Colin was five years old, his family moved to the Bronx, another area in New York City. There they lived in an apartment building with people from many different backgrounds—Irish, Jewish, and Italian. Colin attended school, although he wasn't a very good student. His parents urged him to study, but his lessons did not interest him.

When Colin graduated high school and began college, he did not know what he wanted to do with his life. Then one day he saw a marching drill team. As the **cadets** moved in unison in their crisp black uniforms, they caught Colin's attention. That was it! Colin would become a soldier. He joined the **ROTC** and eventually became the team's commander. He had direction—a goal. Colin's grades improved and he experienced a feeling of confidence and pride in his new successes.

After college, Colin joined the army and underwent **rugged** training courses where he learned things, such as how to parachute and survive in the wilderness. Colin's first assignment was in West Germany. His job was to protect Europe from the powerful Soviet Union. Colin also served in the war in Vietnam. He continued to do his best and prove himself to be a strong leader. He was **promoted** many times. He also married and began a family.

In 1972, after earning his master's degree in business administration, Colin was chosen to serve as a special assistant at the White House. People liked him. He was very organized and **dedicated.** Colin went on to become an assistant to the Secretary of Defense. In 1987, he became President Reagan's national security adviser. Two years later Colin became the first black chairman of the Joint Chiefs of Staff, supervising everyone in the **armed forces.**

General Colin Powell retired from the military in 1993. Through hard work and dedication, Colin accomplished many extraordinary things and earned many honors. He is truly an American hero.

Name ______________________________ Comprehension: critical thinking, recalling details

General Colin Powell American Hero

Directions: Answer the following items. Use another sheet of paper if you need more space to write.

1. Why did General Powell hold frequent newscasts during the Persian Gulf War?

2. How do you think Colin's life in the Bronx helped shape his character?

3. What do you think was the turning point in Colin's life? Explain.

4. Name two of Powell's achievements. Describe how he accomplished them.

5. Tell about a goal you have achieved. How did it make you feel?

6. Define *informed, cadets, ROTC, rugged, promoted, dedicated,* and *armed forces* as used in the article.

Children's Literature

Reading quality children's literature adds to a fourth grader's sense of independence. Since the picture books of second and third grade are no longer a challenge, your fourth grader will most likely welcome new chapter books he can read for himself, at his own pace, and for *pleasure!*

In fourth grade, your child will learn to

- identify different *genres* of literature including biographies, historical fiction, informational books, and poetry
- read a variety of literature including fiction (legends, novels, folklore, tall tales, and science fiction), as well as nonfiction (autobiographies and diaries), plays, and poetry

The list on page 113 is just a fraction of the recommended children's literature for a child in fourth grade. Compiled by librarians, teachers, publishers, and well-respected reviewers, this list has some of the most beloved classics of children's literature, books your child is sure to find engaging, entertaining, and educational. From swashbuckling adventures to tear-jerking coming-of-age tales, the books on this abbreviated list are some of the best tales ever written, for *any* age.

But don't stop there. Explore the appropriate sections of your local bookstore or library. Talk to reference librarians, teachers, or friends to discover the newest, latest classics to add to your list. Better yet, explore the shelves yourself! After all, you know your child's likes and dislikes, interests and hobbies, and hopes and dreams better than any librarian or bookstore clerk. Look below for some ways to add to your own reading list.

Book Club Wish List

Book clubs are a wonderful way to build your child's home library in an affordable and timely manner. When your child brings home those monthly paperback book club forms, look over them together. Let your child create a monthly wish list of several books a month. Depending on your budget, order all of them on his wish list—or just one! Either way, your child will be choosing books you know he will like, and they'll be his to keep—forever.

Get Carded!

A library card is a wonderful way to begin your child's adventure in reading—for free! Make library day a weekly adventure, and return and check out books as often as possible. Making trips to the library fun and enjoyable, rather than a chore, is one sure way to make it a popular destination.

Get Gifted!

Make children's literature a part of holiday and birthday gift giving from now on. Whether it's your child's favorite author in hardcover or a paperback biography of his favorite sports star, your child will come to expect—and enjoy—books as gifts. This is a great way to slowly but surely build a personal library for your child while developing a lifetime habit of reading.

Fourth-Grade Reading List

Abel's Island by William Steig
Ace: The Very Important Pig by Dick King-Smith
All About Sam by Lois Lowry
Beetles, Lightly Toasted by Phyllis Reynolds Naylor
The Best School Year Ever by Barbara Robinson
Bill Peet: An Autobiography by Bill Peet
Catch That Pass! by Matt Christopher
Christina's Ghost by Betty Ren Wright
Coffin on a Case by Eve Bunting
Coyotes in the Crosswalk by Diane Swanson
Dead Letter by Betsy Byars
Dolphin Treasure by Wayne Grover
Encyclopedia Brown and the Case of Pablo's Nose by Donald J. Sobol
Falling Up by Shel Silverstein
Fat Fanny, Beanpole Bertha, and the Boys by Barbara Ann Porte
The Great Brain by John D. Fitzgerald
Hannah on Her Way by Claudia Mills
Harvey's Horrible Snake Disaster by Eth Clifford
Homer Price by Robert McCloskey
Hot and Cold Summer by Johanna Hurwitz
How to Eat Fried Worms by Thomas Rockwell
Hurricanes: Earth's Mightiest Storms by Patricia Lauber
In the Year of the Boar and Jackie Robinson by Betty Bao Lord
Jim Ugly by Sid Fleischman
Knights of the Kitchen Table by Jon Scieszka
Lily's Crossing by Patricia Reilly Giff
Little House in the Big Woods by Laura Ingalls Wilder
The Little Ships: The Heroic Rescue at Dunkirk in World War II by Louise Borden
Lost in the Devil's Desert by Gloria Skurzynski
Matilda by Roald Dahl
Maxie, Rosie, and Earl: Partners in Grime by Barbara Park
Off and Running by Gary Soto
The Paper Airplane Book by Seymour Simon
Pippi Longstocking by Astrid Lindgren
Ramona Forever by Beverly Cleary
A Shooting Star: A Novel About Annie Oakley by Sheila Klass
Soup in Love by Robert Newton Peck
Stinker From Space by Pamela Service
The Twin in the Tavern by Barbara Brooks Wallace
Wanted...Mud Blossom by Betsy Byars
The Whipping Boy by Sid Fleischman
Who Knew There'd Be Ghosts? by Bill Brittain
Windcatcher by Avi

Motivating Reluctant Readers

Some fourth graders just don't get excited about the prospect of *reading*. With all the distractions of video games, TV, movies, and sports, how can anything as simple as reading a book compare? While every student must read various textbooks in class and for homework, many students feel that time off from school means time off from reading. Combine this with a lack of books directed specifically at this age group, and you have a recipe for nonreaders. Making books accessible, available, and attractive is a parent's responsibility.

To ensure that your household is reader-friendly, here are a few questions you can ask yourself:

- Are there books on your nightstands and coffee tables?
- Does the number of TVs outweigh bookshelves?
- Is there a dictionary in the house?
- Is your child overscheduled with afterschool activities?
- Do you each have your own library card?

Motivating a fourth-grade reader is not as challenging as you might think. Children often take their cues on such matters from their peer and family groups. If *you* consider reading a chore, it may be hard to get your child to read as time goes by. So let your child see you reading! Read all kinds of materials! Read together and discuss what you are reading. Go to a movie *and* read the book!

Below are a few ways to get your child to read more often, and enjoy doing so.

Any Words Will Do

Who says that all reading has to come from a book? Encourage your child to read by starting small. Sports magazines, comic books, trading cards, and even the backs of cereal boxes are all steps in motivating your child to read more. For a reluctant reader, any words devoured throughout the day are a small victory in the war against reluctant reading.

The Family That Reads Together...

Got a reluctant reader? Get the family involved by making reading a household, or family, activity. Turn off the TV one weeknight, and pull out a good book to read aloud to your fourth grader. After a while, let him read to you. Make the night a weekly tradition, and your child's interest in reading may grow by leaps and bounds.

Movie Madness!

Many fourth graders need just a small push to turn reading into a fully blossomed passion. Why not take note of the movies or TV shows your child enjoys so much? Then check out or purchase the novelization of that movie or TV series and present it to your child. The motivation to read will already be there, as will the interest level. So taking the first step is often as easy as going to the movies!

Answer Keys

Page 6
1. ceiling
2. weird
3. receive
4. aisle

Page 7
From: **Jeannie**27@email.com
To: Petey14@yourmail.org

Dear Pete,
My **teacher** took my class on a **field** trip yesterday. We went to a farm and fed the **turkeys** and chickens oats, grains and **peas**. My friend and I got to hold a **monkey**. That was **really neat**. The weather was beautiful, so we stayed all day. When it was time to **leave**, no one wanted to go. Once we got on the bus, I put my head back and fell **asleep**. I had **peaceful dreams** of my great day!
Jeannie

Page 8
boat
crow
goat
oar
flow
float

Page 9

Blue Eyes	Green Eyes
child	dye
wild	my
mild	dry
Yellow Eyes	by
light	
bright	**White Eyes**
tight	any
might	weight
night	every
	easy

Page 10
It will not be **smooth** sailing for you boat lovers today. You'll have to **choose** an indoor sport. It's **true** that winds **blew** at 25 knots this morning and will **continue** to blow even stronger as the day wears on. So, no **cruising** today! A **few** of you may want to repair your sails instead. The Coast Guard will be on alert to **rescue** any sailors in distress.
So, stay tuned and **view** the **news** tomorrow to see if you and your **crew** can sail the deep **blue** sea in the near future. This is Sailor Sam, in my **new** sailor **suit**, signing off.

Page 14
1. strange
2. ages
3. knew
4. nearly
5. no
6. tragedy
7. edges

Page 16

benches	watches	desserts	boxes
bushes	families	daisies	pebbles
donkeys	valleys	glasses	tigers
countries	beaches	roses	

Page 17
loaves, shelves, themselves, knives, leaves, gloves, scarves, thieves, wolves, wives, lives

Page 18
Corrected plurals: women, children, oxen, mice, geese, feet
Our hot-air balloon adventure began early in the morning. We jumped out of bed at 4:00 AM when the alarm went off. We wanted plenty of time to drive to the farm and meet with our flight instructor and crew. Take-off was scheduled for sunrise. It was chilly, so we dressed in **pants** and jackets. As the sun came up, the beautiful balloon was inflated, and we were ready to go. We anxiously climbed into the gondola. In addition to the pilot, there were two **women** and two **children** on board. The pilot gave the signal, and the **people** on the ground let go of the ropes.
As the balloon lifted higher and higher, I could see the roof of the barn and two **oxen** standing nearby. I think I even saw two **mice** running toward the barn. We floated silently above the large farm, passing over a field where **sheep** were grazing. As we climbed over the mountain, we spotted several **deer** and **elk** in a meadow below. When we drifted toward a lake, we saw ducks in the marshes and two **moose** in the distance.
We felt like we were walking in the clouds. The rest of the world was just over the horizon. But, like all good things, our journey had to end. We landed beside the lake where our spotter crew and a gaggle of **geese** greeted us. What a great day! It was good to have our **feet** on the ground.

Page 19

3
1. zero **zeroes**
2. zoo **zoos**
3. potato **potatoes**
4. tomato **tomatoes**
5. hero **heroes**

6
1. knife **knives**
2. tooth **teeth**
3. thief **thieves**
4. wife **wives**
5. shelf **shelves**

1
1. suitcase **suitcases**
2. rock **rocks**
3. flower **flowers**
4. egg **eggs**
5. sandwich **sandwiches**

4
1. donkey **donkeys**
2. strawberry **strawberries**
3. daisy **daisies**
4. butterfly **butterflies**
5. candy **candies**

8
1. saleswoman **saleswomen**
2. grandchild **grandchildren**
3. ox **oxen**
4. foot **feet**
5. hand **hands**

2
1. box **boxes**
2. lunch **lunches**
3. goose **geese**
4. dish **dishes**
5. kiss **kisses**

5
1. turkey **turkeys**
2. donkey **donkeys**
3. key **keys**
4. birthday **birthdays**
5. library **libraries**

7
1. moose **moose**
2. elk **elk**
3. sheep **sheep**
4. mouse **mice**
5. deer **deer**

Page 20

1. That giant gorilla is (**meaner**, meanest) than his father.
2. The large lion in the back is the (louder, **loudest**) of all the lions in the zoo.
3. The playful monkey in the middle is the (cuter, **cutest**) monkey of the bunch.
4. The laughing hyena was the (funnier, **funniest**) animal that we saw today.
5. My favorite animals are the giraffes. They are the (cooler, **coolest**) animals of all.
6. On the way home, I fell asleep (**faster**, fastest) than my friend Tommy.

1. big	<u>bigger</u>	<u>biggest</u>
2. hot	<u>hotter</u>	<u>hottest</u>
3. thin	<u>thinner</u>	<u>thinnest</u>
4. flat	<u>flatter</u>	<u>flattest</u>
5. red	<u>redder</u>	<u>reddest</u>
6. fat	<u>fatter</u>	<u>fattest</u>

7. The elephant was the **biggest** animal in the zoo.

Page 21

1. Several **women** went shopping for **shoes** and spent **hundreds** of dollars.
2. My **cousin** is a real **beauty**. Her **height** is five feet eight inches, and she has long blonde hair and a **heart** of gold.
3. My uncle played the lottery **twenty** times and finally **won** a **million** dollars.
4. The concert I attended was filled with **forty thousand young people**.
5. We went to an **island** that was **thirty**-three miles away. It was in the middle of a **beautiful** blue **ocean**.
6. Someone left this chocolate brownie. Do you know **whose dessert** this is?
7. **Arithmetic** is my favorite subject. I love to work with **decimals** and all kinds of **numerals**. Do you?
8. I **sure** like math and multiplying three-**digit** numbers. What is your favorite subject?
9. I often help my brother **answer** social studies **questions**, so he doesn't have to **guess**. Whom do *you* help?
10. I love **sugar** cookies. I could eat **eighteen** or **nineteen** of them. How about you?

Page 25

For many years, people have said there's a large dinosaur-like monster living in Loch Ness in Scotland. Throughout the last 100 years, an **endless** series of sightings of a monster in the deep lake has been reported. Like the mysterious Bigfoot creature, the existence of the Loch Ness monster, better known as Nessie, has sometimes been supported by fuzzy photo images. The **truthfulness** of this evidence is disputed.

Nessie is usually seen swimming in the **darkness**. Although a dinosaur of her size would be very heavy, the water makes her seem **weightless**. No one knows for sure if she exists. Those who think they have seen her sometimes feel **hopeless** because of the lack of real evidence. **Needless** to say, they may only find **happiness** when they finally encounter Nessie face to face or, at least, get others to agree that Nessie exists.

1. endless, truthfulness, darkness, weightless, hopeless, needless, happiness
2. Answers will vary.

Page 26

When my neighbor, Mr. Poltergeist, had to leave town **unexpectedly** on business, he asked my friend Becky and me to take turns walking his dog, Boo. We decided **agreeably** that each of us would walk Boo once a day. There was just one problem with this **agreement**. The first time I went to Mr. Poltergeist's house, I spotted a sign and gasped in **astonishment**. The sign on the front door said, "Beware of the dog!" I don't scare **easily**, but I was **definitely fearful** to open the door alone. I called Becky and told her the situation **nervously.** We decided to walk Boo together, and I **secretly** breathed a sigh of relief.

Later that day, Becky and I arrived at the house prepared to win Boos friendship with dog biscuits. We wore our running shoes just in case. After finding the hidden key, we opened the door **hopefully**. We were greeted **eagerly** by a big black Lab. We **quickly** placed the leash on Boo, and he bounded **happily** down the street. He was quite a **playful** dog. **Luckily** we had a strong leash. It was an **achievement** just to hang on as he pulled us **powerfully** down the street. There was no way to run **gracefully**. After several blocks, we were **totally** exhausted. **Finally**, we brought Boo back home, **thankful** to be alive. We opened the door **quietly** and looked inside **carefully**. We saw **suddenly** to our **amazement** that the house was **hopelessly** haunted!

1. unexpectedly	6. definitely	11. eagerly	16. achievement	21. thankful
2. agreeably	7. fearful	12. quickly	17. powerfully	22. quietly
3. agreement	8. nervously	13. happily	18. gracefully	23. carefully
4. astonishment	9. secretly	14. playful	19. totally	24. suddenly
5. easily	10. hopefully	15. Luckily	20. finally	25. amazement
				26. hopelessly

Page 27

teach teacher
count counter
skate skater
visit visitor
drive driver
preach preacher
design designer
counsel counselor

1. singer
2. reader
3. painter
4. counter
5. actor
6. helper
7. builder
8. photographer
9. writer
10. biographer

Page 28

There are many types of jellyfish, but one of the deadliest is the sea wasp, or marine stinger. The body of this box-type jelly can get as big as a basketball with up to 60 tentacles hanging down as long as 15 feet! These jellyfish are not aggressive though. They don't have to be. They swim up to five miles per hour—pretty quickly for a jellyfish—dangling their long tentacles in the surf behind them. Then something, usually a fish, gets caught up in their tentacles.

The tentacles of a jellyfish are practically invisible. This is where the stinging cells, called **nematocysts,** are located. The poison in these cells kills their prey almost instantly. This prevents the helpless victim from struggling and thrashing the jelly's delicate tissue. Since the prey is now defenseless, the jelly can take its time devouring its meal. The tentacles are quite helpful for the jellies, but quite deadly for those who get tangled in their "webs."

deadliest
hanging
dangling
stinging
helpless
struggling
thrashing
defenseless
devouring
helpful

Page 29

Steven Spielberg has always had a great imagination. As a child, he would rearrange the furniture and pretend to be on a movie set. As he grew older, his family told him to grow up! Luckily, he never really did. He continues to use his imagination to make motion pictures. Spielberg has made many amazing feature films. Have you seen *ET*, *Raiders of the Lost Ark*, *Jurassic Park*, and *Back to the Future*? In each of his action movies, Spielberg pays attention to details. Before shooting, he is on a mission to choose the best location. He may look at many places in many nations.

In addition, Spielberg has to think about weather conditions and nature. Heavy rains will stop production. Muddy roads and thick jungles cause problems with transportation. Wild animals and pesky insects are trouble! Special-effects experts plan carefully for stunts. These crews must use extra caution on the set. Actors and stuntmen get careful instructions on what to do and when to do it. A new movie sensation takes shape under Spielberg's direction! Who knows what creatures Spielberg will feature in his next adventure?

Page 30

1. We were in a state of disbelief when the magician made the woman vanish into thin air.
2. We were unable to get the safe open.
3. After the mission, the pilot had to debrief the colonel.
4. He had to repay the loan with interest.
5. Explain the report so everyone can understand it.
6. No one could decide which car was the safest. They all seemed to disagree.
7. Retrace your steps to see where you left your keys.
8. She is very sweet. She never has an unkind word to say about anyone.
9. I heard her exclaim from the back of the room that she knew the answer.
10. The exterminator needed to debug the whole house when the back door was left open for a week.
11. He had to exchange the pair of shoes for ones that fit.
12. It's hard to undo a bad habit that you have had for a long time.

Page 31

Circled Word	**Prefix**
disappeared	dis-
reentered	re-
unselfishly	un-
rearranged	re-
unsteadily	un-
regained	re-
reconsidered	re-
disappointed	dis-
disobeyed	dis-
unconcerned	un-

Root Word	**Suffix**
appear	-ed
enter	-ed
selfish	-ly
arrange	-ed
steady	-ly
gain	-ed
consider	-ed
appoint	-ed
obey	-ed
concern	-ed

Page 32

1. blueberry	blue	berry
2. cornbread	corn	bread
3. airstrip	air	strip
4. sunlight	sun	light
5. snowman	snow	man

Some of the possible compound words:

newspaper
storybook
sailboat
rainfall
cloudburst
silkworm
bluebird
flashlight
newsflash

Page 33

Dr. Howard Carter gazed spellbound through the doorway. He saw armloads of riches. Six hard years of digging led to this great discovery. He would wire Lord Carnarvon with the good news. Carnarvon, a British nobleman had paid for Carter's trip.

Carter had discovered the underground tomb of an Egyptian king. The tomb dated back to 1300 B.C. It was the first Egyptian tomb found undamaged. Grave robbers had not taken anything. Footstools, chairs, jewels, necklaces, earrings, and other riches filled Carter's view. Nearby were the king's chariots, his hunting bow, and even his sandals. Ancient Egyptians were always buried with their favorite belongings.

News of Carter's 1922 discovery was broadcast on radio stations. Newspaper headlines captured the interest of people everywhere. Years later King Tutankhamen's tomb still remains the most well-known archaeological find in history.

A. Build Word Skills Circle each compound word in the story.

B. Expand Your Vocabulary Find two words in each sentence below that you can turn into a compound word. Write the word in the blank provided.

1. They are keeping the Egyptians' relics in a safe place. **safekeeping**
2. Walk this way to view the mummy. **walkway**
3. Dr. Carter wrote a note about his findings in his book. **notebook**
4. The body of Tutankhamen had some decay. **somebody**
5. A collar shaped like a wreath was placed on the mummy. **wreathlike (collarlike, mummylike)**
6. Egyptians believed in a life after death. **afterlife**
7. Burial tombs were built under the ground for pharaohs. **underground**

Page 34

1. united
2. greatly
3. connecting
4. largest
5. powerful
6. continuous
7. manual
8. lengthy
9. protection
10. warrior(s)
11. ruler(s)
12. nomadic

Page 35

A.

1. pre-
2. uni- or mono-
3. fore-
4. tri-
5. uni- or mono-
6. dis- or un-
7. peri-
8. en-
9. un- or dis-

B.

1. against
2. two
3. beside
4. in favor of
5. again
6. into
7. back
8. across, over

Page 36

A. Build Word Skills

1. Islam **Islamic**
2. far **afar**
3. gleam **gleaming**
4. empire **emperor**
5. price **priceless**
6. palace **palatial**
7. attract **attractive**
8. love **beloved**
9. beauty **beautiful**
10. perfect **perfection**
11. majesty **majestic**
12. science **scientists**

B. Expand Your Vocabulary

	meaning	word root	another example
1.	with; along with; together	**sym**	**sympathy, symphony, symptom, synchronize*, synthetic***
2.	measure	**meter**	**kilometer, perimeter, barometer, thermometer, diameter**
3.	breath, live	**spir**	**respiration, conspirator, expire, transpire, spirit**
4.	know	**sci**	**conscious, scientific, science, conscience, conscientious**
5.	write	**graph**	**autograph, paragraph, graphite, biography, graphic**

* The word roots *sym* and *syn* have the same meanings.

Page 37

A. Build Word Skills

1. power: dynam
2. end: fin
3. earth: geo
4. break: fract
5. believe: cred
6. remember: mem
7. law: leg
8. great: magn
9. to be born: nat
10. number: num

B. Expand Your Vocabulary

1. enumerate: to count
2. magnify: to enlarge
3. legal: lawful
4. geography: science of the earth's surface
5. dynamo: generator; energetic person
6. fraction: a type of number; a piece broken off—fragment
7. credible: worthy of belief
8. final: coming at the end
9. nativity: birth
10. memo: a written reminder

Page 38

1. small
2. smart
3. hate
4. accident
5. alike
6. awful
7. foolish
8. enormous
9. continue
10. decorate
11. delicate
12. weak
13. funny
14. spoon
15. copy
16. necessary
17. everlasting
18. repair
19. danger
20. thoughtful

Antonyms left in the jar: *nervous* and *confident*

Page 39
Answers will vary. Possible answers:
see: look, notice, glimpse, watch, view
broad: wide, spacious, large, big, thick
bright: brilliant, lustrous, radiant, shiny, gleaming
perilous: dangerous, risky, hazardous, treacherous, unsafe
watched: looked, observed, regarded
glare: light, blaze, dazzle
bursting: exploding, popping, blasting, erupting, flaring
banner: flag, pennant, streamer
free: independent, self-governing, unconfined, unrestrained
home: abode, place, dwelling, residence, shelter

Page 40
- drugstore, apothecary, pharmacy: places where medicines are dispensed
- exposition, show, exhibition: places where works of art are publicly shown
- roused, stirred, evoked: caused to be called forth or up
- unspoiled, idyllic, picturesque: a state of being charming or quaint
- exceptional, unusual, extraordinary: a state of being beyond the ordinary or usual

Page 41
1. synonyms
2. antonyms
3. antonyms
4. synonyms
5. synonyms
6. synonyms

loathsome: disgusting, repulsive
pulpit: place in a church where a sermon is delivered
pondered: considered thoroughly
vision: something seen in a dream or trance
protest: describing strong objections to (adjective)
vivid: very clear and sharp

Page 42

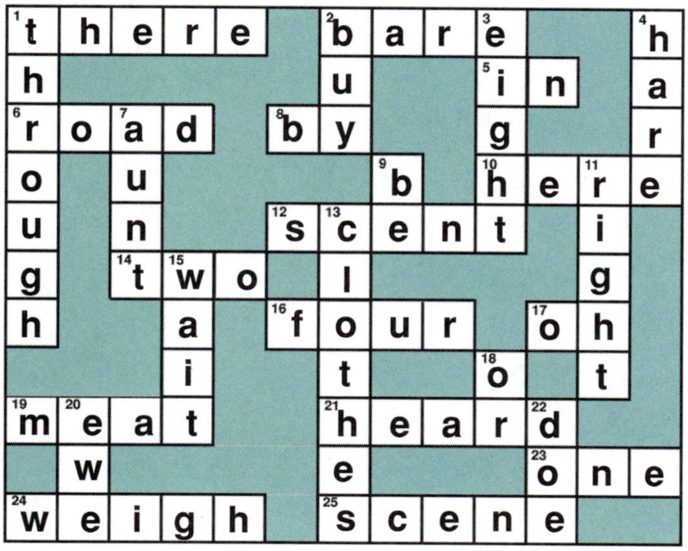

Page 43
1. sea
2. bow, break
3. route, be, there
4. boy, told, some, night
5. guessed, son, not, know, made
6. Choose, or, wait, for, week, By
7. All, through, chilly, night, blew, scent, air
8. prayed, Our, sail, hole, feat, too, for, why
9. course, time, size, would, wear, would, be, for, board
10. Right, soar, flowers, tide, piece, wood, by, eye, new, tale

Page 46
1. E
2. C
3. H
4. A
5. F
6. D
7. I
8. G
9. B
10. J

Page 49
1. Frantic Freddie foolishly fumbled the football.
2. Scouts scratched the scarecrow's scalp.
3. Jake joyfully juggled the jack-o'-lanterns.
4. Randy's rusty rake required repair.
5. Has Helen helped handle Harvey's hefty harvest?
6. Silly squirrels scamper and scurry about in September.
7. Lots of leaves lost their lovely luster.
8. Classy Clyde is clad in colorful clothing.
9. Wednesday's wet weather went westward.
10. Private Polly's patch produced prize pumpkins.
11. Teachers told Tammy to talk on the topic of tomatoes.
12. Bob bought both of Barb's bound books.

Page 50

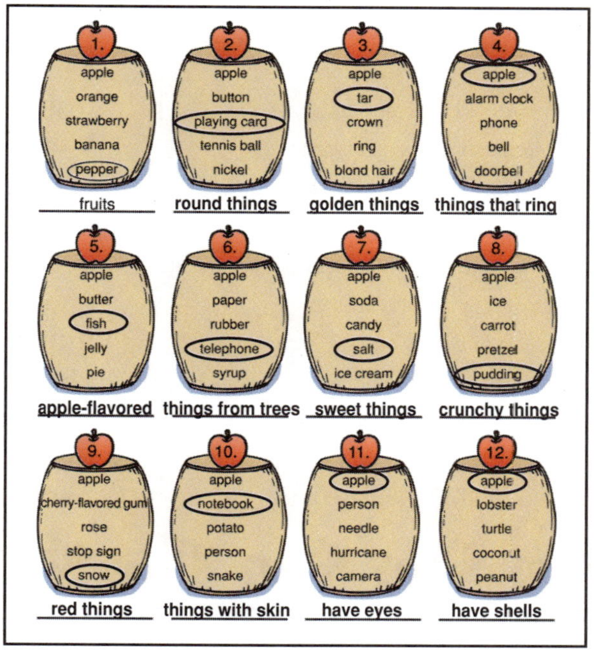

Page 51

1. *Heart* is to *circulation* as *stomach* is to **digestion**.
2. *Rodent* is to *mammal* as *beetle* is to **insect**.
3. *C* is to *Celsius* as *F* is to **Fahrenheit**.
4. *Incisor* is to *cut* as *molar* is to **grind**.
5. *Elephant* is to *tusk* as *rattlesnake* is to **fang**.
6. *Moon* is to *satellite* as *Earth* is to **planet**.
7. *Lunar* is to *moon* as *solar* is to **sun**.
8. *Oxygen* is to *inhale* as *carbon dioxide* is to **exhale**.
9. *Drizzle* is to *downpour* as *flurry* is to **blizzard**.
10. *Buffalo* is to *mammal* as *alligator* is to **reptile**.
11. *Lobster* is to *shell* as *trout* is to **scales**.
12. *Cabbage* is to *leaf* as *carrot* is to **root**.
13. *Galaxy* is to *star* as *forest* is to **tree**.
14. *Butterfly* is to *nectar* as *mosquito* is to **blood**.
15. *Spider* is to *invertebrate* as *whale* is to **vertebrate**.
16. *Bee* is to *swarm* as *wolf* is to **pack**.
17. *Brain* is to *nervous system* as *artery* is to **circulatory system**.
18. *Wood* is to *solid* as *air* is to **gas**.

Page 52

1. *Duck* is to *waddle* as *frog* is to **hop**.
2. *Hot dog* is to *eat* as *milk* is to **drink**.
3. *Water* is to *wet* as *desert* is to **dry**.
4. *Pickle* is to *sour* as *candy* is to **sweet**.
5. *Boat* is to *water* as *airplane* is to **sky**.
6. *Skin* is to *humans* as *scales* are to **fish**.
7. *Flour* is to *wheat* as *sawdust* is to **wood**.
8. *Dog* is to *bark* as *cat* is to **meow**.
9. *Perfume* is to *nose* as *music* is to **ears**.
10. *Potato* is to *vegetable* as *apple* is to **fruit**.
11. *Grass* is to *green* as *sky* is to **blue**.
12. *Spaghetti* is to *Italian* as *taco* is to **Mexican**.
13. *Baseball* is to *throw* as *soccer ball* is to **kick**.
14. *Curtains* are to *windows* as *sunglasses* are to **eyes**.
15. *Apple* is to *skin* as *nut* is to **shell**.
16. *Foot* is to *big toe* as *hand* is to **thumb**.
17. *Shower* is to *bathroom* as *refrigerator* is to **kitchen**.
18. *Lawyer* is to *courtroom* as *teacher* is to **classroom**.
19. *Noise* is to *loud* as *whisper* is to **quiet**.
20. *Smell* is to *nose* as *touch* is to **hand**.

Page 54
1. dentist, credit, lettuce
2. comments, progress, suggests, success, market, insect
3. traffic, cactus
4. comments, progress, contact, products

Page 58
1. Sue caught the keys. Sue gave **them** to Sean.
2. Sue and Sean drove to the store. **They** bought a newspaper.
3. Sue wanted to look up the movie times. **They** didn't start for an hour.
4. Sean was hungry. **He** ate before the movie.
5. Sue and Sean picked up a few friends on the way. **They** all had a great time.

John loves to go to the beach. He (John) could go every day. He (John) loves to surf and walk on the beach. One day, while surfing, a shark went under his (John) surfboard. It (shark) scared him (John) enough to keep him (John) away from the ocean. John realized that **sharks** won't bother him (John) unless they (sharks) are hungry. "Boy," thought John when he (John) got back on the beach, "That scare would really make a great movie!"

Page 59
Nouns
1 pheasant, queen, turnips, bread
2 pie, dinner, platter, quinces, apples
3 tarts, nuts, dates, pie, lunch
4 Great Hall, feast, fish, sausage, fowl
5 cider, brook, manor, orchard
6 Lady Margaret, Devonshire, Sunday, table, delights
7 custards, fireside, Edward, game, chess

Adjectives
1 fond, tender, warm, white
2 Meat, appetizing, hungry, sugary, cooked
3 tastiest, mincemeat
4 royal, certain, freshest, savory, finest
5 refreshing, trickling, apple
6 sumptuous
7 Young, grueling

Page 60
Answers will vary.

Page 61
1. B
2. A
3. B
4. B
5. A
6. A
7. A
8. B

Page 63

gallop	be	see	leap	understand
is	think	explode	was	save
run	carried	jump	wall	grew
will	flew	am	sleep	were
eat	are	wonder	life	sun

Page 64

	Where	How	When
1. The stove temperature should be fairly hot.	A	**F**	L
2. This first pancake is completely burned!	B	**C**	M
3. Oh, no! The batter has spilled everywhere.	**A**	W	Q
4. The king is terribly fond of fresh berries on his pancakes.	P	**R**	V
5. Pancakes must be flipped properly.	X	**Y**	I
6. This pancake is almost done.	E	**L**	H
7. The king often eats three or more stacks of pancakes.	S	K	**E**
8. Chocolate chip pancakes are quite tasty.	J	**U**	G
9. The king is positively picky about his pancakes!	A	**V**	Z
10. I always cook my pancakes to perfection!	T	O	**Y**
11. Here is a new stack.	**E**	C	A
12. A batch of fresh pancakes will be made tomorrow.	M	K	**R**

Write the letter that you colored for each number shown below.

V E R Y C A R E F U L L Y !
9 11 4 5 2 3 12 7 1 8 6 6 10

Page 66

Susan Johnson
310 grave ave
Cape Canaveral, FL 32391
Grave Ave.

Jane Doe
4510 Lester Ct.
merritt island, fl 42891
Merritt Island, FL

Dr. Drey
45 Diamond Rd.
Las Vegas, nv 85021
NV

Jerry Parker
36 Young Ave.
orlando, fl 36298
Orlando, FL

Page 67

1. Mr. Rogers
2. Sen. Richard
3. Dr. Zhivago
4. Miss Sara J. Burns
5. Ms. Helen Rita
6. Gov. Doppler
7. Senator (or Sen.) Johnson will be speaking at my party.
8. Ms. Mariah Carey will be singing my favorite song.
9. Doctor (or Dr.) Doolittle will be performing with animals.
10. Marvin the Magician will be doing magic tricks.
11. Mr. Magoo will be drawing caricatures of all the guests.
12. Governor (or Gov.) Sparkler will be setting off fireworks at the end of the night.

Page 72

Correct (tortoise) sentences:

2. Cindy loves chocolate, but Katie prefers vanilla.
4. To help me be less nervous, Mom practiced my speech with me.
6. Shelby asked Mark, Brendan, and Maya to be on her team.
9. Diane, I'm sorry I didn't laugh at your joke.
10. What day will you be here, Caleb?
13. Mr. Yountz, the best coach in the league, spoke to our class.

Incorrect (hare) sentences:

1. My dad loves to cook and, my mom loves to fix cars.
   Corrected: My dad loves to cook, and my mom loves to fix cars.
3. Even though I forgot to remind her Lea still studied for the test.
   Corrected: Even though I forgot to remind her, Lea still studied for the test.
5. I packed a pen a pencil case and two books in my backpack.
   Corrected: I packed a pen, a pencil case, and two books in my backpack.
7. Yes we will be home on Friday, night.
   Corrected: Yes, we will be home on Friday night.
8. Oh did the game start already?
   Corrected: Oh, did the game start already?
11. I've been expecting you Larry since 5:00.
   Corrected: I've been expecting you, Larry, since 5:00.
12. Billy the funniest kid, in our class has read 11 riddle books.
   Corrected: Billy, the funniest kid in our class, has read 11 riddle books.
14. A huge furry animal is at the back fence!
   Corrected: A huge, furry animal is at the back fence!

Page 73

1. Jerry was reluctant, but he rode the roller coaster with his friends.
2. Susan bought popcorn, candy apples, and hot dogs there.
3. John asked the conductor, "Can you speed up the train?"
4. "No," said the conductor politely.
5. Everyone had fun at the carnival, but all good things must come to an end.

Dear Diary,

Yes, I had the greatest day today. It was my eleventh birthday, and I ate cake, ice cream, and pizza! All my best friends were there, but Sarah didn't show up. That left Ashley, Kate, Loretta, Keisha, Sally, and Pam. What a crowd! Everyone had a great time, but I think we all ate too much. People said, "Oh my stomach hurts" as often as they said, "Happy Birthday." Next year I think I'll skip the pizza—no, maybe the ice cream!

Page 74

2. iguana's tree
3. spiders' web
4. turtles' stream
5. bird's branch
6. eel's darkened crevice
7. children's pride
8. fox's den

Page 75

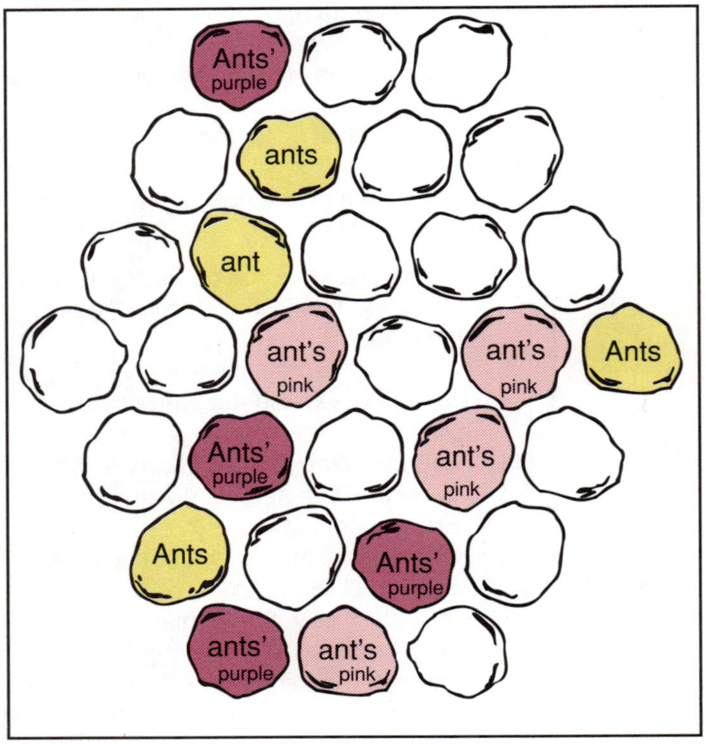

Page 76

I'd	its
it's	body's
There's	It's
They're	I'll
Sightings	shark's
humans	sharks'

Page 77

1. "The silk in my web is so strong that even the heavy dew of a spring morning cannot damage it," said the spider.
2. "I," said the puma, "can jump 12 to 15 feet straight up into a tree!"
3. The polar bear bellowed, "My thick coat keeps me warm while I enjoy a good springtime sparring."
4. "I use my stomach as a table," remarked the sea otter. "I place a rock on it so I can break open clam shells to get to the meat inside."
5. "During the spring and summer, I have about 300 spots that cover my coat so wolves, bears, and other prey can't see me as easily," replied the fawn.
6. "Don't you know that I faithfully follow my mother wherever she goes?" questioned the duckling.
7. "I eventually leave the pond and turn into a frog!" cried the tadpole.
8. "Cooling off on a warm spring or summer day is easy," commented the bird. "I dip my feet and legs into cool water."
9. The bee answered, "I help pollinate many beautiful flowers."
10. "I've been called the world's finest engineer," barked the beaver. "I build dams more than 8 feet high and 40 feet wide."

Page 79

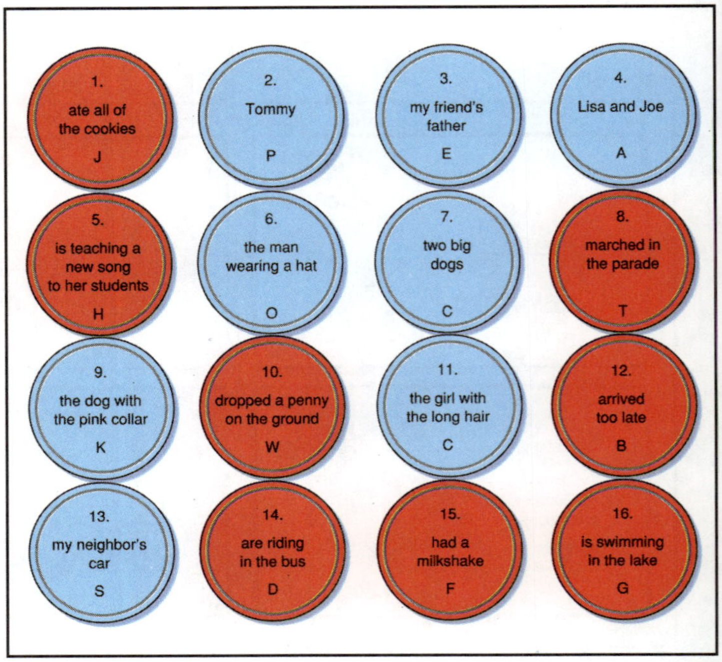

1. ate all of the cookies J
2. Tommy P
3. my friend's father E
4. Lisa and Joe A
5. is teaching a new song to her students H
6. the man wearing a hat O
7. two big dogs C
8. marched in the parade T
9. the dog with the pink collar K
10. dropped a penny on the ground W
11. the girl with the long hair C
12. arrived too late B
13. my neighbor's car S
14. are riding in the bus D
15. had a milkshake F
16. is swimming in the lake G

Page 80

Subjects: L, S, I, P, R, W, U

Predicates: N, C, K, C, E, I, H

Compound Predicates: Tonight's Special is CHICKEN!

Page 81

1. S Peter ate breakfast.
2. R I ate too much food I feel so sick.
3. S The chef prepared our meal.
4. C Corie likes spaghetti, but I would rather eat pizza.
5. R I like to cook I don't like to clean up the kitchen.
6. S My friend from school is eating dinner with us tonight.
7. S Warm milk makes me sleepy.
8. C You like french fries, but I prefer mashed potatoes.
9. S Carrots and peas are my favorite vegetables.
10. R Grandma baked a cake I had a piece of it.
11. S Grapes grow on a vine.
12. C Some apples are red, but bananas are yellow.
13. C Turn on the oven first, and then let it heat up.
14. C We can make lunch, or we can go out to eat.
15. R I dropped my ice-cream cone the clerk gave me a new one.
16. S My little brother ate breakfast and went outside to play.
17. S My fork and spoon dropped on the floor.
18. R I ordered a hamburger the waitress brought it to me.
19. C I ate all of my dinner, and Mom let me order dessert.
20. R I made a pizza it had cheese and pepperoni on it.

Simple

1 3 6 7

9 11 16 17

Sum: 70

Compound

4 8 12

13 14 19

Sum: 70

Run-On

2 5 10

15 18 20

Sum: 70

Page 82

	Agree	Disagree
1. (Sally and Sam) surf from sunrise to sunset.	B	Q
2. (Hamburgers) tastes terrific when served hot off a grill.	C	E
3. (We) roller-skate regularly near Rolling Rock River.	P	F
4. (Wanda) water-skis wonderfully.	R	L
5. (The Higginses) hikes high in the mountains each summer.	K	S
6. (Gertrude) grow wildflowers in her garden.	D	N
7. (I) rides horses at The Triple R Ranch.	Y	A
8. (Bailey) watches birds in his backyard.	Z	G
9. (Carmen) camps at her cousin's country cabin.	M	H
10. (Terrel) travel on a tour bus throughout Texas.	V	J
11. (Sabrina) says sunbathing is simply sensational.	U	X
12. (Five friends) fish at Fairview Farm.	I	B
13. (They) pack a picnic of pasta and pickles.	O	W

Write the letter that you colored for each number shown below.

SUMMER IS A SUPER SEASON!

5 11 9 9 2 4 12 5 7 5 11 3 2 4 5 2 7 5 13 6

Page 83

The order may vary. The following are suggested answers.

1. All of Principal Smith's wastebaskets need to be emptied.
2. Visitors to the White House want to meet the president and the first lady.
3. Seven custodians are needed to take care of Washington School.
4. Tourist sites in Kentucky include Churchill Downs and Mammoth Cave.
5. The Lions Club is sponsoring a German festival in August.
6. Mom and Dad will fly on Delta Airlines to Alaska.
7. One popular beach was devastated by Hurricane Floyd.
8. Three hundred Write-Right pencils were never sharpened.
9. Cousin Carl always brings us fresh Georgia peaches.
10. The Pittsburgh Pirates and the Chicago Cubs hope to play in the World Series.
11. Jack and Evelyn will cross the Atlantic Ocean with their parents.
12. My favorite summer foods are California grapes and Maine lobster.

Page 84

School Of Dessert Science Application

Date: October 14 1998

Name: Chef I Wannabe

Address: 3515 Doughnut circle (Street)

Hershey (City) Pa (State) 20202 (Zip)

Education		
	Name Of School	Location Of School
High School	Trifle High	Sweet Home oregon
College	University Of Sweetwater Station	Wyoming

References:

1. Chef Boy R. Dee (Name) — 232 Spaghetti boulevard (Address)
2. Mr D. Hines (Name) — 101 Cakeleaf Lane (Address)

Previous Experience:

1. I was the pie sli cer at miss Sweettree's bakery
2. last year i delivered frozen (deserts) (two) the local grocery stores.

Why do you want to attend the School Of Dessert Science?

Ive always wanted to (bee) a world famous dessert chef. I want to (lern) how to prepare delicious pies puddings, and Cakes.

Signature: *Chef Wannabe* Date: *October 14, 1999*

Page 86

A.
- 1 Jennifer washed her hands with the new soap.
- 3 Finally, Jennifer sat down to eat dinner with her family.
- 2 Then she dried her hands.

B.
- 2 First I asked for a hamburger and fries.
- 3 Then I changed my order to chicken fingers.
- 1 After I arrived at the restaurant, I looked at the menu to help me decide what to order.

C.
- 1 Jan bought a bag of candy.
- 3 Then she removed several pieces of candy and resealed the bag.
- 2 She opened the bag carefully.

D.
- 1 We have several events planned for the picnic.
- 3 Then we are going to have a relay race.
- 2 First we are going to have a pie-eating contest.

E.
- 3 Finally, he will put his clothes in the soapy water.
- 2 Next he will add some detergent.
- 1 James is going to turn on the water to wash his dirty clothes.

F.
- 2 We celebrate it by having cake and ice cream.
- 1 Jake's birthday is an important day for our family.
- 3 Afterwards we play games.

The	order	of
A	B	C
events	is	important
D	E	F

Page 88

N	1. Koalas are the cutest animals of all.
I	2. The koala is a marsupial—or pouched—animal.
S	3. Koalas make their homes in trees.
M	4. Koalas seem to be happy animals.
A	5. Eucalyptus leaves do not have a good taste.
A	6. The average koala bear needs more than a pound of eucalyptus leaves every day.
E	7. Koala babies are funny-looking animals.
L	8. The word *koala* comes from the word *kaloine* which means "do not drink."
O	9. Koalas are always very friendly.
U	10. The koala gets its water from the eucalyptus leaves that it eats.
A	11. Koalas sleep 18 to 20 hours a day.
R	12. The female koala raises her young alone.
T	13. Once a baby koala becomes too heavy for its mother's pouch, she shifts the baby to her back.
C	14. Everyone who has a chance to see a koala will like this animal.
P	15. Koalas should be used as the next Olympic mascot.
A	16. Eucalyptus trees grow in Australia.

Unscramble the letters on the eucalyptus leaves that you colored to find out where koalas live. Spell this location in the blanks below.

A U S T R A L I A

Page 87

Accept reasonable answers.

3 Use a shovel to remove the grass, but keep all other plants.
Use a shovel to remove the grass and other plants that cover the site.

10 Water your garden so much that the soil never gets dry.
Water your garden when the soil gets dry.

5 Add fertilizer after you have raked the soil smooth.
Add fertilizer after breaking up the soil.

2 Find a site with the proper sunlight.
Many flowers and most vegetables need a large amount of light to grow well.

4 Dig up the soil no more than 8 inches.
Dig up the soil 8 to 12 inches.

9 Plant vegetables in irregularly shaped groups so they can be cared for more easily.
Plant vegetables in straight rows so they can be cared for more easily.

1 Choose a site where the water will keep the soil soggy.
Choose a site where the soil won't get soggy.

8 Space the seeds closely together so they don't grow all over the place.
Space the seeds apart so the plants will have enough room to grow.

7 Choose plants that grow well in any climate.
Choose plants that grow well in your climate.

6 Draw a sketch of your garden after it grows to check for any mistakes.
Draw a sketch of your garden before planting to avoid making mistakes.

Page 89

Predictions will vary, but possible responses include the following:

1. Jennifer does not do well on her science test.
2. Liz's mother tells her she cannot go walking until she finishes her chores.
3. To earn money for the theme park, Michelle gets a job baby-sitting and Dave gets a job cutting grass.
4. Ray and Andrew realize that they are lost.
5. Sharon's hair is too curly. *Or* Sharon's hair was damaged because the perm solution was left on too long.

Page 90

Causes

1. Since the new hurricane was the fourth of the season, **it was named *David.***
2. The cloud was tall, dark, and anvil-shaped, **so we knew it was a cumulonimbus cloud.**
3. Because we had a blizzard warning, **we made sure we had blankets and food in the car before driving to town.**
4. Since the storm was called a *typhoon,* **I knew that it wasn't located in the United States.**
5. Storm surges were predicted when the hurricane hit the coast, **so we evacuated the island.**
6. Because thunderstorms pump lots of hot air from the earth's surface high into the air, **they are called earth's "air-conditioning system."**
7. Since we have no basement, **my family gathers in the bathroom in the center of our house during a tornado warning.**
8. Because Hugo was such a terrible hurricane, **that name will never be used again.**
9. Whenever I hear thunder, **I know there has been lightning.**
10. We spotted a tornado while driving in a car, **so we stopped and took cover in a deep ditch.**
11. Since the tornado was classified as an F-5, **we knew houses and cars had been blown away.**
12. There were 15 seconds between when I saw lightning and then heard thunder, **so I knew the storm was three miles away.**

Page 91

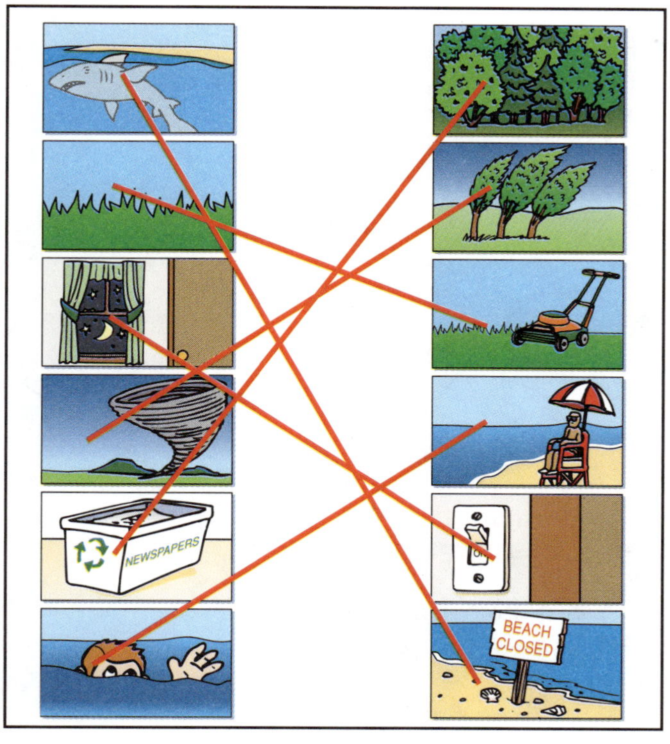

Page 92

Answers will vary, but here are some suggested answers:

1. T Michael Jordan is an unbelievable athlete.
2. F Michael won Rookie of the Year in 1982 in high school.
   Michael won Rookie of the Year in 1984 in the NBA draft.
3. F Michael played for 14 years and felt he still had to prove himself.
   He played for 14 years and felt he had nothing more to prove.
4. T He said that the media had made his life intolerable.
5. T Michael then played baseball for a short time.
6. F Michael returned to basketball on March 19, 1993.
   Michael returned to basketball on March 19, 1995.
7. F It took no time at all to get back up to speed.
   It did take time to get back up to speed.
8. F Michael didn't win that many games for the Chicago Bulls, even though he was a great player.
   He did help his team win a lot—171 games.

Page 93

foot stove	1. This portable tool was used during colder months. It was a pierced metal box often mounted on wooden legs. A colonist placed hot coals inside, then put his feet on top of it to keep warm.
wool cards	2. This tool was used to gather wool for spinning. It was made of thin rectangular boards with handles. Each board had a leather strip filled with wire teeth. The wool was collected by brushing the tool across a sheep, then scraping the boards together to roll the wool into balls.
spinning wheel	3. This tool helped colonists make cloth for clothing. A foot pedal was used to turn a wheel that spun the wool or flax to be made into cloth.
wooden churn	4. This tool was a wooden container with a long handle. Butter was made by pumping cream up and down in it.
corn pestle	5. Corn was a staple of the colonial diet. Colonists used this bowl and stick to grind corn into flour. It was similar to the tool used by pharmacists to grind medication.
warming pan	6. Colonists took the chill out of a cold bed with the help of this tool. It was a circular metal pan with a long wooden handle. The pan was filled with coals from the fire, then moved quickly between the bed's covers to heat them up.
toasting rack	7. This tool was an iron rack on stilts or legs. A colonist would place bread in the rack, then use its long handle to put it near the fire. The stilts kept it just above the hot coals.
Betty lamp	8. This tool was used for light. A colonist filled its container with grease or oil, then lighted the wick placed in its small spout. Its hook and chain allowed it to be hung where needed.

Page 94

1. *Newsprint*—coarse paper made from wood pulp on which newspapers are printed.
   Newspapers are printed on/coarse paper made from wood pulp.
2. *Tabloid*—a smaller-sized newspaper that has lots of pictures, larger headlines, and shorter articles than a standard paper.
   half the size of a standard newspaper's pages/lots of pictures, larger headlines, and short articles.
3. *Beat Reporters*—reporters who cover news in one particular location or about one particular subject.
   Reporters who cover news in one particular location or about one particular subject are called beat reporters.
4. *Lead*—the first paragraph of a news story.
   the first paragraph, which contains important facts.
5. *Copy Editor*—person who checks a reporter's article for accuracy, writes a headline for it, changes some words to make it easier to understand, or cuts some of it if it is too long.
   someone who checks it for accuracy and writes a headline for it. This person may change some words to make the article easier to understand or cut some information if the story is too long. The person responsible for this job is called a copy editor.
6. *Layout*—a sketch.
   a layout—or sketch—of each newspaper page/where each story, picture, and advertisement will be placed on a page.

Page 95

1. daring
2. preserved
3. X
4. grope
5. thriving
6. saltpeter
7. channels
8. rich
9. ventured
10. hands
11. extend
12. hardy
13. recesses
14. succeeded
15. tuberculosis
16. immensity
17. labyrinth
18. X
19. X
20. eerie

Page 96

Answers will vary, but here are some suggested answers:

1. He is courageous, not a quitter, has great endurance, and is strong.
2. by not letting the accident get him down, by overcoming his great obstacles
3. He works hard to make public appearances and continue with his work.
4. No, he continues to make public appearances, direct, and act.
5. Yes, he won't stop until he can walk and hug his son again.
6. Answers will vary.

Page 97

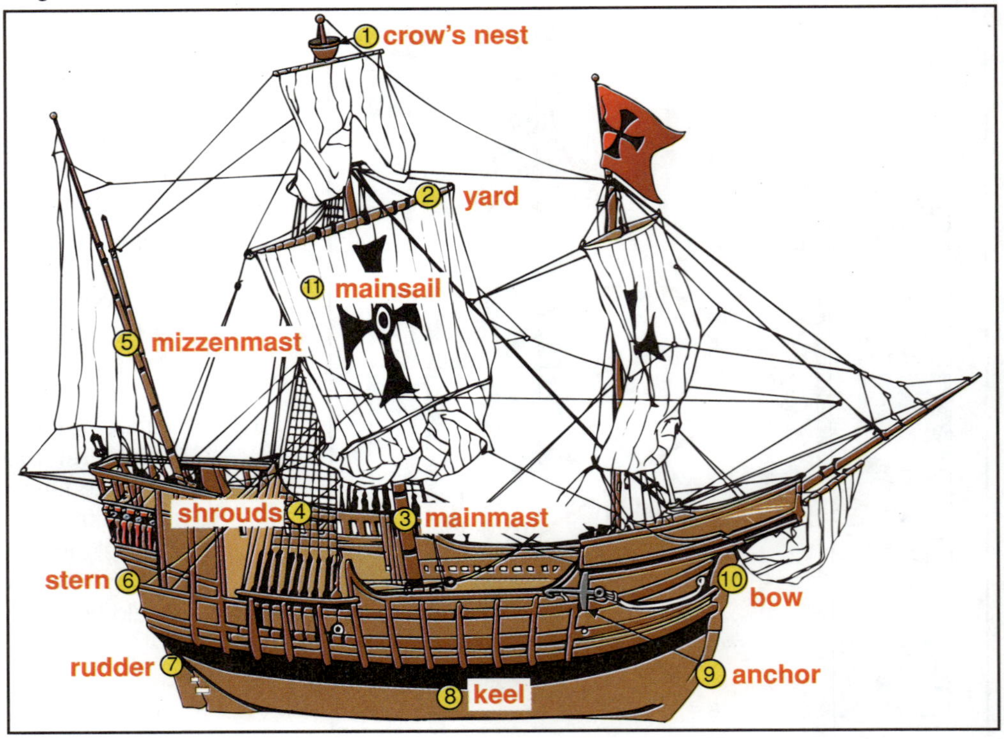

Page 98

1. moderate gale or near gale
2. whole trees sway; walking against wind is difficult
3. 39–46 mph
4. light breeze, light air, calm
5. 47 mph
6. slight structural damage occurs, such as signs and antennas blown down
7. calm
8. 5 mph
9. strong gale, whole gale or storm, storm or violent storm, hurricane
10. more than 74 mph

Page 99

1. –18°F
2. The temperature decreases (gets colder) by 6°F (from –18° to –24°).
3. –86°F
4. –53°F
5. The temperature increases (gets warmer) by 4°F (from –53°F to –49°F).
6. 15 mph
7. 20°F
8. –5°F with 30 mph winds = –56°F wcf
   –15°F with 10 mph winds = –40°F wcf
   The lower (colder) wcf is –56°F.
9. 10°F with 30 mph winds = 33°F wcf
   –5°F with 15 mph winds = 38°F wcf
   –25°F with 5 mph winds = 31°F wcf
   The highest (warmest) wcf is –31°F.
10. Answers will vary. Possible pairs include
    30 mph winds with 25°F temperature = –10°F wcf
    20 mph winds with 20°F temperature = –10°F wcf

    35 mph winds with 35°F temperature = 4°F wcf
    20 mph winds with 30°F temperature = 4°F wcf

    40 mph winds with 35°F temperature = 3°F wcf
    10 mph winds with 20°F temperature = 3°F wcf

    40 mph winds with 30°F temperature = –5°F wcf
    15 mph winds with 20°F temperature = –5°F wcf

Page 100

1. 1901–1910
2. 1931–1940
3. the Great Depression
4. 1941–1950
5. 3,100,000
6. increased
7. 1981–1990
8. 1931–1940

Try This: about 418,889 immigrants *(The total number of immigrants should be divided by 90 years since it counts all of 1901 through the end of 1990.)*

Page 101

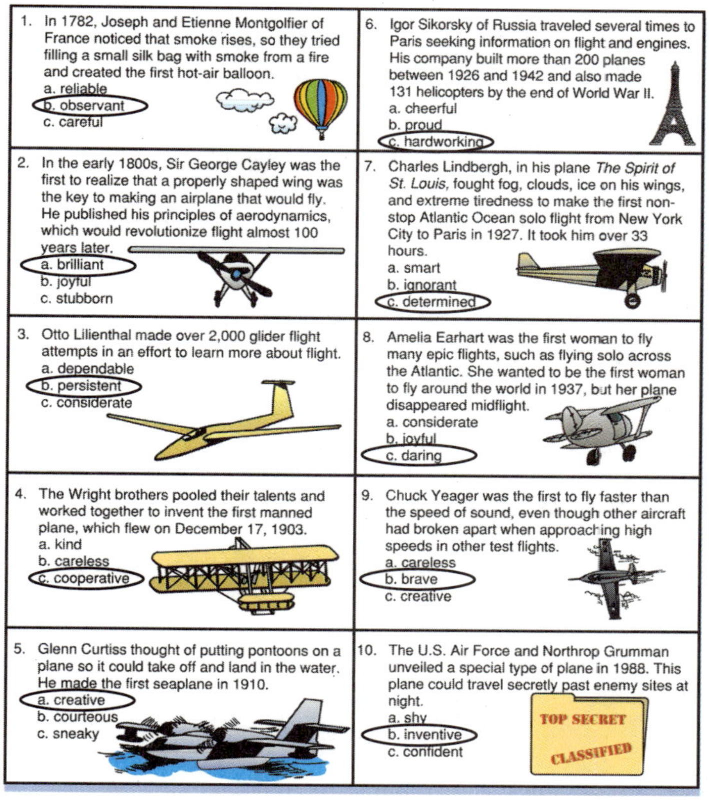

1. In 1782, Joseph and Etienne Montgolfier of France noticed that smoke rises, so they tried filling a small silk bag with smoke from a fire and created the first hot-air balloon. a. reliable b. observant c. careful	6. Igor Sikorsky of Russia traveled several times to Paris seeking information on flight and engines. His company built more than 200 planes between 1926 and 1942 and also made 131 helicopters by the end of World War II. a. cheerful b. proud c. hardworking
2. In the early 1800s, Sir George Cayley was the first to realize that a properly shaped wing was the key to making an airplane that would fly. He published his principles of aerodynamics, which would revolutionize flight almost 100 years later. a. brilliant b. joyful c. stubborn	7. Charles Lindbergh, in his plane *The Spirit of St. Louis,* fought fog, clouds, ice on his wings, and extreme tiredness to make the first non-stop Atlantic Ocean solo flight from New York City to Paris in 1927. It took him over 33 hours. a. smart b. ignorant c. determined
3. Otto Lilienthal made over 2,000 glider flight attempts in an effort to learn more about flight. a. dependable b. persistent c. considerate	8. Amelia Earhart was the first woman to fly many epic flights, such as flying solo across the Atlantic. She wanted to be the first woman to fly around the world in 1937, but her plane disappeared midflight. a. considerate b. joyful c. daring
4. The Wright brothers pooled their talents and worked together to invent the first manned plane, which flew on December 17, 1903. a. kind b. careless c. cooperative	9. Chuck Yeager was the first to fly faster than the speed of sound, even though other aircraft had broken apart when approaching high speeds in other test flights. a. careless b. brave c. creative
5. Glenn Curtiss thought of putting pontoons on a plane so it could take off and land in the water. He made the first seaplane in 1910. a. creative b. courteous c. sneaky	10. The U.S. Air Force and Northrop Grumman unveiled a special type of plane in 1988. This plane could travel secretly past enemy sites at night. a. shy b. inventive c. confident

Page 103

1. Medical care is better today because we have vaccinations to prevent many diseases. There also have been many medical advances to help premature babies live.
2. Polio is a disease of the central nervous system. It affects a person's muscle control.
3. Wilma overcame the physical challenge of having a crippled leg.
4. Wilma's experiences early in her life probably gave her greater courage and determination.
5. Wilma was given the nickname Skeeter because she was always "buzzing around."
6. Answers will vary. She probably feared poverty, illness, and racism.
7. At the 1960 Olympics, Wilma was the first American woman to win three gold medals.
8. In the article *prematurely* means "happening too soon"; *diagnosed* means "recognized as having a disease or condition"; *persisted* means "kept on doing something in spite of obstacles"; *resolute* means "strongly determined to do something"; and *racism* means "believing that one particular race is better than others or treating people unfairly because of their race."

9–10. Answers will vary.

Page 105

1. The earth is compared to a mote of dust floating in the morning sky. Carl's comparison helps create a clear mental image—that the earth is a speck of dust floating in the sky.
2. Carl was very inquisitive and determined. He had a great imagination and an interest in the world around him.
3. Carl observed the stars at night, asked questions, and read books as a young boy. He studied physics and astronomy in college.
4. In the article, *fired* means "filled with excitement or enthusiasm"; *quest* means "an act of seeking"; and *extraterrestrial* means "existing outside the earth or its atmosphere."
5. Carl read books by Jules Verne and H. G. Wells.
6. Answers will vary. Having knowledge in a variety of areas helped Carl tackle many different topics.

7–9. Answers will vary.

10. A *theory* is a hypothesis, or educated guess, explaining observable facts.

Page 107

1. The best title for this article is *B—A Missionary To The Poor.*
2. In the article, *sari* means "a long piece of light material wrapped around the body and over one shoulder"; *devoted* means "gave time, effort, and attention to"; *missionary* means "someone who is sent by a church or religious group to teach that group's faith and do good works"; *convent* means "a building where nuns—women who devote themselves to God—live and work"; *slums* means "overcrowded, poor, and neglected areas of housing in cities or towns."
3. Mother Teresa was honored with the Nobel Peace Prize for her work with the poor.
4. Mother Teresa's early experiences probably influenced her later life by helping shape her religious beliefs and teaching her the importance of helping those who are less fortunate.
5. After Mother Teresa decided to become a missionary, she moved to a new country, leaving her family and friends; she joined a convent where she received religious training and learned a new language.
6. Mother Teresa felt that God wanted her to leave the convent to live with and serve the poorest of the poor.
7. Mother Teresa began the Missionaries of Charity, which provided food for the needy and ran hospitals, schools, and shelters for the poor.
8. When Mother Teresa said, "Calcutta can be found all over the world if you have eyes to see," she probably meant that if we would just look around, we would see that there are poor people everywhere who need our help.

Page 109

1. Estefan and her parents left Cuba because Fidel Castro came into power.
2. Gloria was often the only Latina in her class.
3. *tempo:* the rate or rhythm of a musical piece; *croons:* sings in a soft, soothing voice; *native:* where someone was born; *exiles:* people forced to leave their homeland
4. The band crossed over from the Latin music market into the American pop music market.
5. Many immigrants come to the United States seeking economic opportunities, as well as political and personal freedom.
6. Answers will vary.
7. Many Cubans have settled in Miami because it is so close to Cuba.
8. Gloria and her parents were *refugees* from Cuba. A *Latina* is another name for a Hispanic-American girl. Estefan has become famous as a *soloist.* Estefan is *Hispanic* because she is of Cuban heritage.

9–10. Answers will vary.

Page 111

1. General Powell held frequent newscasts during the Persian Gulf War because he wanted Americans to know about what was happening.
2. Colin's life in the Bronx probably helped shape his character by helping him get along with people from many different backgrounds and understand that despite ethnic differences, all people are equal.
3. The turning point in Colin's life was probably when he joined the ROTC. It gave him a goal and helped him experience confidence and success.
4. Answers may vary. Possible achievements include the following: He helped our country achieve victory during the Persian Gulf War. He worked hard to become a good soldier. He continued his education, earning a master's degree. He rose to the highest position in the military. He was the first Black American to head the Joint Chiefs of Staff. He accomplished these achievements through hard work and dedication.
5. Answers will vary. Accept reasonable responses.
6. In the article, *informed* means having information, being educated about something; *cadets* means young people who are training to become members of the armed forces; *ROTC* means Reserved Officers' Training Corps; *rugged* means harsh or difficult; *promoted* means moved up to a more important job; *dedicated* means giving a lot of time and energy to something; and *armed forces* means all of the branches of a country's military, including the army, navy, air force, marine corps, and coast guard.